Teaching Music in Primary Schools

Patrick Jones and Christine Robson

LearningMatters

KT-573-813

First published in 2008 by Learning Matters Ltd.

British Library Cataloguing in Publication Data
A CIP record for this book is available from the British Library.

ISBN 978 1 84445 141 8

Cover design by Topics
Text design by Code 5 Design Associates Ltd
Project management by Deer Park Productions, Tavistock
Typeset by Pantek Arts Ltd, Maidstone, Kent
Printed and bound in Great Britain by Bell & Bain Ltd, Glasgow

Learning Matters Ltd
33 Southernhay East
Exeter EX1 1NX
Tel: 01392 215560
info@learningmatters.co.uk
www.learningmatters.co.uk

Practical Handbooks **Achieving**

QTS

Teaching Music in Primary Schools

Contents

Contents

Acknowledgements

The authors would like to thank all of those primary trainee teachers on the BA and post-graduate courses over the years who have inspired or contributed classroom stories.

Special thanks are due to Manor Park Primary in Cheshire for permission to take photographs of music making in the school but also to the Key Stage 1 team for classroom case studies.

Thanks are due to Delph Primary School and St Hugh's C of E Primary School for the contribution about instrumental music and choir work in their school.

Introduction

Why would you be reading this book? You are probably already well into your teacher training/education programme. Music may only have a small general place in your undergraduate or postgraduate programme but you may see it as one of a range of foundation subjects that you would like to focus on at this time. Your programme may additionally offer music within options, electives and/or specialisms or you may have encountered it through some cross-curricular experience and observed it being taught in school. However, you have experienced music you now wish to have more secure knowledge, understanding and skills. In this book we acknowledge the very varied musical backgrounds that trainees will have and present a range of basic know-how, snapshots of good practice and exercises in self-development to enable you to acquire the understanding, knowledge and skills you need to teach music in a primary school or Early Years setting with some confidence.

Firstly, you will need to review the part that music plays in your own life as the basis on which to build.

REFLECTIVE TASK

Learning objective: To have begun a process of self-auditing by recalling your own musical experience.

Make notes on the following.

- Is listening to music an important activity for you and is it largely solitary or do you ever go to events, concerts or clubs to hear music?

- Do you listen to or experience music as part of events that you attend for other purposes?

- Are you knowledgeable about styles of music?

- Do you take part in any music making, as a player, singer, technician or dancer?

- Now consider how these experiences could be starting points for working musically with children.

- What are your musical areas for development?

Most adults experience music through listening to recordings. Some may sing informally (e.g. at football matches) or formally (e.g. in church) and yet others may have continued the school experience of playing and singing in amateur music groups. A few will have written songs or belong to a group that creates its own music. However, these three types of musical activity embody three of the core skills of the music curriculum: listening, performing and composing. By undertaking the self-auditing process above you will find that you do have expertise in some area of music and this is the point on which to build your music-teaching confidence.

However, you will also bring a particular attitude to teaching music that can help or hinder your practice.

The emotional baggage that you carry associated with music education in your past may be negative and if so this needs to be jettisoned through the skill building exercises and positive images of music teaching that follow.

REFLECTIVE TASK

Learning objective: You will have recalled your own musical experience and established a personal view of what 'being musical' means.

Summarise your own music education experience under headings of positive and negative. Consider carefully the positive aspects and how you may apply those features in your own approach to teaching music. Finally summarise what you believe being musical means especially in relation to teaching in school.

The conventions for written music used in this book

You may well not be a fluent reader of music notation and you may not have very much musical experience. On the other hand you may be a very competent performer. Some performers may not use notation; some others may have a little knowledge of notation; and yet others will have used notation when playing an instrument at school. In order to address the different needs we will use three different systems of notation. For rhythms without pitch we will use a simple rhythm notation convention first used by the Hungarian music teacher and composer Zoltán Kodály and hope that non-readers can pick this up fairly quickly.

We will generally keep to simple rhythms made up of two note values:

- Whole notes notated as **I** and
- Half-notes notated (in a pair) as **⊓**

A useful way of remembering these is to call whole notes 'tea' and two half-notes 'coffee'.

Hence would be notated as: *tea coffee tea tea*
I ⊓ I I

For songs or melodies we will use two systems. The first will be letter names of notes by the words they apply to, for example in this Ghanaian song:

This conveys some of the contour of the melody also.

Thirdly, we will give the Western notation convention for songs so that those of you who do read a little can use this and those who don't will at the very least get the general idea. We will try to use well-known melodies when possible and write the letter names above the notes. In doing this we have created our own system to make clear the difference between a low c and a high c. There is a convention commonly used in textbooks about music but it would entail use of letters with additional tags which for our purposes would be unnecessarily complicated. So our convention reads as follows:

For the notes most commonly used in the classroom, 'c up to b', we use normal lower-case letters, for below that capitals, and above italic.

Finding your way in the book

The subject of music in education defies breaking down into clearly defined subsections and so the use of chapters with topic headings has led to a little duplication and some splitting up of one topic in order to maintain the coherence of another. So, for example, it is that the use of electronic keyboards is mentioned in three different places in order to ensure that the list of instruments is complete, the topic of composing has an important ICT component and ICT is included in the range of cross-curricular links with music. We have also cross-referenced in order to enable these split components to be connected.

For all references to recorded music see Appendix 5.

1
An overview

By the end of this chapter you should:

- **know enough about the background to music in the school curriculum to understand current practice in British primary schools;**
- **understand how music education is practised in relation to the broader curriculum and the school day;**
- **understand how music may contribute to a range of current concerns and initiatives.**

This chapter addresses the following Professional Standards for QTS:
Q1.2, Q2.1, Q2.2, Q2.5, Q2.6, Q2.7, Q3.1, Q3.2, Q3.3, Q3.4, Q3.5

Historic background to the music curriculum in British primary schools

Introduction

To bundle all the Foundation subjects together, as they often appear to be, and to treat them as if they all have equivalent status, structures and functions is a great mistake. Some subjects have a strong body of knowledge and some skills, e.g. history, others are principally about developing skills and understanding, e.g. design and technology and drama has a place largely as a learning methodology. Like design and technology education, music education is primarily about developing skills and understandings. Sometimes music teachers have tried to make their subject conform to the more general pattern of having a body of knowledge and, perhaps, avoided too much problematic classroom management by sitting children down to learn about music. This does not reflect the real nature of the subject, which is essentially about experiencing music. Prior to the introduction of the National Curriculum in 1989 there were only variable guidelines and traditional wisdom about what this experience should be. There was always plenty of singing, often strongly supported by radio and television broadcasts. However, despite the interest in creativity that arose in the late 1960s only a little composing went on and listening to recorded music was not seen as a formal component except at secondary level. Music always had a status as an important aspect of school life and hence had a role presenting a public face of the school. This tended to provide a special place for the more talented children. However, when the National Curriculum was introduced at last there was an entitlement set down for all children of a richer, more multifaceted music curriculum that was an integral part of the school curriculum.

Varied contributions to the music curriculum

The twentieth century saw great changes in general educational practice and music education was no less subject to developments and fashion. In the late nineteenth century the educational forum, the National Education Association, included a music section which is evidence that music was recognised as having a part in primary education in Britain. In fact it had been since the establishment of general publicly funded education. At this time most of the ideas about teaching methodologies focused on singing since this was the primary if not the only musical activity. Hence the methods first developed by pioneers of music education in this country such as Sarah Glover and later John Curwen and accepted by the English Education Department in 1860 were to support amateur singing with a simple form of music notation.

Figure 1.1 Sarah Glover (1785–1867)

This system, known by the French name of 'sol-fa', gave names to each of the seven notes:

Doh, Re, Mi, Fa, Soh, La, Ti

These days the system is better known as the subject of a song from the *The Sound of Music*, i.e. 'Doh a deer, a female deer'. I imagine few of us these days would want to model our teaching on the rather grim look of Sarah Glover's teaching style and yet the method has greatly influenced more recent music educators, among whom has been the Hungarian music teacher and composer Zoltán Kodály.

Kodály's approach to music education was based on teaching, learning and understanding music through the experience of singing. The musical material he proposed that teachers should use was the folksong of the teacher's own country. Music skills were and, indeed, are to this day learned using the sol-fa system through the written names and additional hand signals. Other key music educators also adopted the system and then developed their own particular take on this by giving emphasis to different aspects.

One of these teachers was Emile Dalcroze, a Swiss musician who developed a method of teaching music building on responses to music through physical movements. His method is commonly known as Eurhythmics – yes, some older readers will remember this as a pop group name!

Both of these educators have their dedicated followers to this day, but probably the most influential of all these pioneers was Carl Orff, who is best known as the composer of the choral work *Carmina Burana* but who has been far more influential throughout the world through the adoption of his ideas for creative music-making in classrooms. He designed a series of child-friendly classroom instruments based on African and Indonesian originals which would enable children to learn to play or create simple melodies without years of building up technique. These instruments will be familiar to all British children as the standard instruments to be found in every classroom. Furthermore, Orff also adopted, as indeed did Kodály, the use of a scale, which is commonly found in folk music, the pentatonic or five-note scale. These two major innovations, he believed, enable children to draw on inherent musical abilities both rhythmic and melodic in a natural but also structured way.

How do children experience the music curriculum in contemporary British primary schools?

We should start by looking at how the music curriculum is implemented by drawing on your own general experience. You have already summarised your broad musical experience but now you need to focus on primary school music.

PRACTICAL TASK PRACTICAL TASK PRACTICAL TASK PRACTICAL TASK PRACTICAL TASK

Lerning objective: You will begin to understand how music education is practised in relation to the broader curriculum and the school day.

List under the headings below all the places, times and purposes of musical activities that you have both observed and heard about in any of the periods you have spent in primary schools.

Listening to recorded music
Singing
Chanting
Using instruments
Instruments combined with singing
Use of actions and body sounds

If you really have searched out every memory of music in primary schools you may well have listed some of the following.

- In assembly: listening to recorded music, singing religious songs
- In dance lessons: listening to recorded music or to hand-held instruments
- Songs to begin and end the day
- Songs to assist memorising, e.g. tables
- Music to assist understanding, e.g. counting songs, foreign language songs
- Music class lessons
- Individual or group music lessons, e.g. recorders, choir, violin.

Hence it will be apparent that music activity takes place in a variety of places and con-texts with a range of purposes and all of this should be pulled together to compile a comprehensive view of the music curriculum. However, whether purposefully or not, there is a framework into which most of this will fit.

The National Curriculum for music

In the National Curriculum (2000) there are four key musical skills: performing, compos-ing, appraising and listening.

- Controlling sounds through singing and playing – **performing skills**;
- Creating and developing musical ideas – **composing skills**;
- Responding and reviewing – **appraising skills**;
- **Listening and applying knowledge and understanding.**

You will find that the progression from Key Stage 1 to Key Stage 2 is expressed in some additional requirements.

- In section 1a Key Stage 1 children are expected to use their voices expressively by singing songs and speaking chants and rhymes. But in Key Stage 2 they should sing songs, in unison and two parts, with clear diction, control of pitch, a sense of phrase and musical expression.
- In section 3 (appraising skills) there is the additional requirement at Key Stage 2 for children to analyse and compare sounds.

PRACTICAL TASK PRACTICAL TASK PRACTICAL TASK PRACTICAL TASK PRACTICAL TASK

Learning objective: To become conversant with the structure of the National Curriculum for music and the progression from Key Stage 1 to Key Stage 2 in particular.

Photocopy the 'Knowledge and skills' page for Key Stage 1 and Key Stage 2. Cut out the four sections on each page and place the Key Stage 1 and Key Stage 2 versions alongside each other. Note where the differences lie. Pencil in the key differences for each section that will have implications for you.

Elements of music

Listening, composing and performing have already been part of the discussion but apprais-ing is new. This is the 'understanding' part of the curriculum in that it gives importance to reflecting on and evaluating music. In order to do this, children do need to know some terms with which to describe what they are hearing. Hence the key concepts of music are spelled out in the curriculum document as the elements of music listed below.

- Duration – short and long notes, pulse (or beat), and rhythm.
- Dynamics – loud /quiet / silent.
- Tempo – fast and slow.
- Timbre – the quality of sound, affected by the way instruments are played and the material of which they are made.
- Texture – the layers of music, the way sounds are combined.
- Structure – the way sounds are organised in time.
- Pitch – high and low, melody.

There are some differences in the way aspects of the Key Stage 1 and Key Stage 2 curricula are described. For instance, at Key Stage 2 the term 'gradations' is used when describing pitch and dynamics so that it is clear that children should be perceiving and using more precise differences in these two elements.

Many of the *Special Seven*, as they might be known, are exemplified in one activity which could be a regular part of music lessons of a Key Stage 1 class.

Teaching example

A call-and-response chant led by the teacher.

T:	Have you brought your *happy* voice?	
Ch:	Yes I've brought my *happy* voice	Timbre
T:	Have you brought your *quiet* voice?	
Ch:	Yes I've brought my *quiet* voice	Dynamics
T:	Have you brought your *quick* voice?	
Ch:	Yes I've brought my *quick* voice	Tempo
T:	Have you brought your *high* voice?	
Ch:	Yes I've brought my *high* voice	Pitch

In addition, the call-and-response form of the chant is a distinctive structure and hence five out of the seven elements are being explored in this one activity.

The teacher gives a lively performance of *happiness or quietness* in her voice which the children readily imitate. As they do this they get used to the elements of music which when altered change the character of the composition or performance.

Each of the musical elements can be exemplified as the focus of a short activity.

Teaching examples

1. Duration (rhythm)
   Children choose instruments that can sound continuously, such as a rattle, maracas or guiro. They are given a picture (graphic score) as follows.

   Their activity is to create a musical performance based on the long and short notes indicated.

2. Dynamics – Key Stage 2
   Children are shown the writing below on an interactive whiteboard (IWB)

   # 1234Mary's at the cottage door

   They are directed to read the rhyme out loud together, speaking loudly or quietly as indicated by the size of the letters. The teacher leads by counting the children in.

3. Pitch – Key Stage 1
   The children imitate the teacher as she pretends to catch a sound in her hand, e.g. an *ooh* sound, and takes it on a journey up-and-down with her hand. Her voice follows the up-and-down movement of her hand. The children imitate her actions and sounds.

---

4. Tempo – Key Stage 1 or 2

   The children accompany with appropriate speed chanting the rhyme:

   Slowly, slowly, very slowly   Quickly, quickly, very quickly
   Creeps the garden snail   Runs the little mouse
   Slowly, slowly, very slowly   Quickly, quickly, very quickly
   Up the garden rail.   Round and round the house

5. Texture – Upper Key Stage 2

   The class listen to a standard pop song and identify which instruments and voices are playing and when. An instruction might be, *put up your hand when there are only two instruments playing together*. When a child identifies a point in the music, the teacher asks which instruments the children think are playing.

6. Timbre – Key Stage 2

   Children are asked to choose instruments and to select particular sounds from those instruments to accompany a video of wildlife activity in a river.

7. Structure – Key Stage 1 or Key Stage 2

   Children, seated in a circle, take part in a class music-making activity in which each in turn improvises a drum rhythm to a count of four. In between each improvisation the drum is passed on while everyone in the group claps one repeated pattern. This makes a piece in the form or structure ABACADAE, etc.

Work on dynamics, tempo and timbre is developed further in Chapter 4, pitch in Chapter 3 and duration in Chapter 6.

Breadth of study

The final paragraph (Section 5) in the music curriculum refers to teaching methods and choice of repertoire. They are important principles, which:

- hold onto the notion that each music lesson should have a variety of activities in it such that each of the four key activities will be touched on and one or two will be the main focus;
- expect music to be responsive to non-musical as well as musical starting points;
- insist that music, like other subjects, should involve different forms of organisation to enable children to be actively and independently engaged;
- broaden the definition of ICT in music to include the use of electronic recording equipment and instruments as well as computers;
- expect that the repertoire of songs and recorded music to reflect a broad spectrum of genres both historical and cultural.

Musical resources

Like other subjects music requires its own resources. These include sound-makers or sources, spaces in which to work away from other classes, books and forms of recorded music and playing and electronic recording equipment.

This is discussed in greater depth in Chapter 4.

Sound sources

- Voice and different voice qualities.

- Body sounds.
- Instruments: improvised/manufactured acoustic and electronic.

The voice

The voice will always be the primary sound-maker. The government initative the *Music Manifesto* wishes to re-establish singing as the most important skill in the music curriculum. It may have in mind rather more the secondary curriculum in which singing has been eclipsed by the emphasis on use of music technologies. But developing singing skills rather than just singing for recreation is a good goal for primary schools. All children have the capacity to sing and will use this spontaneously in the playground. The expressive capacity of the voice is much greater than that produced on instruments by young children; hence there is more to be learned about music performance through singing. The musical activity 'Have you brought your ... voice?' shows how this range can be explored.

Body sounds

Stamps, clicks and claps make the most natural accompaniments to songs. This can be seen very well in this African greeting song called 'Funge'.

PRACTICAL TASK PRACTICAL TASK PRACTICAL TASK PRACTICAL TASK PRACTICAL TASK

Learning objective: To appreciate how body sounds can be used as a song accompaniment

Try learning the song and then use it in school.

The feet movements are:

    step to the right (with a stamp);
    close the left foot (with a stamp).

The hand movements are:

    clap to the left side;
    clap to the right side.

Above the words are the notes of the song. The spacing indicates how long the notes are.

The children can easily learn a wide range of sounds if you model them in a call-and-response activity such as 'Follow me'.

The teacher demonstrates a continuous body sound, e.g. rapid slapping alternate thighs, and the children join in, then the teacher changes to rubbing hands together and the children copy. Other sounds could be:

- rapid stamping on the floor;
- tapping on the head;
- alternating finger clicking left and right.

These sounds are like natural percussion accompaniment. However, it is worthwhile exploring the sound potential of everyday materials as well.

Improvised or homemade instruments

There are a great number of materials that are either thrown away or can be bought cheaply that make very effective instruments.

PRACTICAL TASK PRACTICAL TASK PRACTICAL TASK PRACTICAL TASK PRACTICAL TASK

Learning objective: To appreciate the potential of everyday objects as sound-makers.

Take three empty food tins or plastic containers of different sizes and tape them together so that the top sides are flush with one another. You have a three-pitched drum which may be played with a stick or piece of dowelling.

Now create a short piece of music with an interesting rhythm just using the three notes.

Manufactured instruments

The majority of instruments used in primary schools are percussion, i.e. instruments that are hit in various ways. They are classified into the groups:

- untuned, i.e. those that play rhythms only;
- tuned, i.e. those that play melodies.

Most of these instruments are the ones referred to earlier that were developed by the music educator Carl Orff in Germany in the mid years of the last century. Here we will focus on untuned instruments. Tuned instruments will be explored in depth in Chapter 4.

Untuned instruments provide rhythm and timbre (or sound colour) to the music and include:

- drums;
- tambourines;
- woodblocks;
- bells;
- rattles.

The variety of these has been extended in recent years by the addition of a range from different musical traditions, e.g. djembe drums from West Africa.

PRACTICAL TASK PRACTICAL TASK PRACTICAL TASK PRACTICAL TASK PRACTICAL TASK

Learning objective: You will begin to understand how resources are organised to support the practice of music education in a primary school.

List the untuned musical instruments you can find in your placement school. Most importantly show where instruments are stored and what implications this has for how music is taught. Create your own classification of the instruments.

Sorting the instruments into categories according to specific criteria can be a useful exercise for young children. For instance, instruments/sound-makers that:

• can make	only short sounds		or only long sounds;	
• are usually	quiet		or loud;	
• are made of	metal,	wood		or plastic;
• make	bright sounds,	tapping sounds	or shaking and rattling sounds.	

The children need to explore the potential of a sound-maker (while treating it respectfully of course) in order to classify it. The quality that they will find most distinctive will be the sound quality, or timbre, of the sound-maker but it may be its potential to vary dynamics or to make short or long sounds. The outcome of the exercise can be some music-making based on the contrast between the groups such as the duration activity above or a whole-class band type activity as follows.

TEACHING EXAMPLE

The teacher divides the class into three groups.

bright sounds	tapping sounds	shaking and rattling sounds

In turn, the children silently pick up a sound-maker from a tray that has been put out on the floor in front of their group. The children have one minute to practise making repeated or long sounds. When all are ready, the teacher directs all the children to have their sound-maker ready to play at a given signal. When the teacher points to the group they start to play their sounds and when she shows them a flat hand they stop. The teacher is able to combine one to three groups together and have periods of silence this way. This way she creates a composition and models how children themselves may be able to direct a composition.

Accommodation

Accommodation for music is not something a trainee has much control over so you may need to be open to a variety of practices in school. An ideal is that every classroom is big enough to accommodate a range of organisations of the class away from desks. The class may be seated on the floor in a circle or horseshoe for class musical activities or split into sub-groups for independent work. In most classes this is not possible without moving the furniture, so music takes place in the hall or in a designated room. This may also be determined by the degree to which noise carries from room to room. The third factor to consider is the availability of resources. Musical instruments, because of their size and expense, need to be shared between classes hence they are housed in the hall or a corridor, usually on a trolley for ease of transport. Some teachers play instruments themselves and if this happens to be a piano then the class needs to go to where the piano is accommodated. However, the piano is not often the most suitable accompanying instrument and therefore its availability should not be the determining factor.

You also need to consider that the music curriculum is broken up into a range of disparate activities taking place in different places throughout the week. Even if the formal music lesson takes place in the hall at a predetermined and booked time, much else will take place in the classroom in an opportunistic way.

Organisation is discussed in greater depth in Chapter 8.

Printed material

Printed material to support music in the primary school is plentiful and you will find much listed in Appendix 4. An important point to consider for those who are less musically experienced is whether these depend on the reader being able to read music. It will be found that these days most song repertoire books are published with an audio CD and so you will be able to learn any songs by ear (perhaps in the car or on the bus on your way to school). Some material comes in the form of progressive schemes of work designed for use throughout a school with comprehensive lesson plans.

Extra-curricular music

This topic will be consider in greater depth in Chapter 8 but at this stage it needs to be clarified that the National Curriculum quite deliberately did not embrace what has traditionally become the larger part of music activity in schools, that is to say extra-curricular music. The purpose of the National Curriculum was to lay down a framework of entitlement for all children and this could only be expected within the formal curriculum. The success of the National Curriculum for music was that all schools had to ensure that this basic requirement was in place and the general curriculum was enriched as a result. The Office for Standards in Education (Ofsted) (2002) reports have commented favourably on the development of the music curriculum in primary schools throughout the 1990s and this judgement was made regardless of extra-curricular music making. However, as the next section in this chapter sets out, that position has shifted in the new century.

The impact of current initiatives on the music curriculum

The Music Manifesto

This government initiative was launched in 2004 by the DfES, has as its aims:

- to provide every young person with first access to a range of music experiences;
- to provide more opportunities for young people to deepen and broaden their musical interests and skills and to identify and nurture our most talented young musicians;
- to develop a world-class workforce in music education;
- to improve the support structures for young people's music-making.

One the most significant means of doing this has been to promote singing in a number of ways and this has and will have quite an impact in primary schools. There will also be the sustaining of funding for instrumental tuition and the encouragement of collaboration between schools.

Every Child Matters

This large-scale government initiative is now behind the reorganisation of education and children's services in every local authority. But most importantly it has led to a rethink about the range of children's entitlements schools should contribute. The five themes, which will probably be very familiar to you, are:

- being healthy;
- staying safe;
- enjoying and achieving;
- making a contribution;
- economic well-being.

Although music may make a contribution in all respects, it has a particular place in 'Enjoying and achieving'. Intuitively we know that music activity raises the spirits of those who take part. The QCA 2004/5 annual report on curriculum and assessment iden- tifies in its first key finding that *The arts make a difference to pupil's well-being, through lifting their spirits and helping them express themselves* (2005, p7). Singing is an essen- tial part of early morning routines in school. In my work as a teacher and music facilitator I know how great a role it has in nurturing community and hence individual mental health. The *Music Manifesto* points to the important role that music has to play in sup- porting the well-being of children and young people. By arguing for music providers to work in partnership with local authority children's services, it sees children and young people having a say in what is made available so that they are what children both need and want. Another relevant example is the promotion of singing in hospitals by the National Network of Arts in Health in order to promote confidence, ability and well-being. Recent research supports these anecdotal arguments on a firmer basis. Damasio asserts that happiness positively affects the way our brains and bodies work (2003).

Excellence and enjoyment and the new Primary Strategy

Under the main heading of this initiative are the subheadings 'Creating a learning culture' and 'The learning environment – routines'. These are key ideas schools are reminded about that create a positive ethos for learning. All music-making, but singing in particular, is important in the creation of this good classroom ethos. The timing of opportunities for singing at key moments of the day such as first thing in the morning and last thing in the afternoon are seen as important ways of helping children to feel good about themselves and their community and helping to structure the day in an enjoyable way. The strategy, exemplified earlier, of using songs or recorded music to accompany routines such as tidying up is used in many Early Years classrooms.

Another heading is 'Key aspects of learning across the primary curriculum', under which are listed aspects of learning which cut across the curriculum boundaries, such as problem- solving and creativity as well as literacy. The special place of music in developing early literacy was first set out in *Progression in phonics* DfES (2001) and has now been updated in the Primary National Strategy – *Letters and sounds* (2006), the first phase of which reads quite as much like a music curriculum as literacy. The contribution that music makes to other areas of the curriculum will be explored in much greater depth in Chapter 7 but it is worth noting that in broad terms music can be considered as a teach- ing methodology or strategy in its own right.

Inclusion and the music curriculum

The British system of education has always had a degree of commitment to inclusive- ness. However, this has been variable in its success. Sometimes it has been expressed in terms of provision of equal opportunity. This has generally been understood to mean that the curriculum should be differentiated where practical for the variable needs of the children in a class. It is worth spelling this out because in France and in some other European countries 'equal opportunities' is expressed quite differently as provision of the same curriculum to all and the same expectations. Hence in Britain it is clear that teachers are expected to understand the different capacities of children to access the curriculum. In other words, it is about equality of learning opportunity. The curriculum is differentiated in order that all children are able to access learning at appropriate levels for their relative capacities to learn.

In more recent times and particularly since the introduction of the Disability Discrimination Act and the government policy of closing separate provision for children with less severe disabilities, inclusion has meant that teachers need to not only differentiate their curriculum but to co-ordinate a team of support staff for children with increasingly diverse special needs. So what does all of this mean for music education?

There does appear to be a tension between such personalising of the curriculum and the need for music to be a group activity. However, children with different needs can contribute fully to a whole-class musical activity in a number of quite natural ways. Although musically experienced children may offer something special in classroom music lessons, this should not make children who have difficulty with, say, pitch (i.e. singing in tune) feel excluded. Within one activity there can be a range of roles. Singing, in particular, with young children should be presented as an inclusive activity.

TEACHING EXAMPLES

The teacher is leading the singing of a round. First she teaches the four lines of the round to the class line by line. She directs the children to listen while she models the singing of a line, then they copy her. She does this for each line and then maybe again in order to consolidate the knowledge of the song. She demonstrates two lines for them to copy and then she demonstrates the whole song. This experience for the children is one of being included in a group experience without any sense of being different even if success is variable. But then the teacher directs a group of children, perhaps those that she has heard are having trouble with pitching higher notes, to sing just the first line of the round repeatedly so that it becomes an *ostinato* (the musical term for a repeated pattern). She then adds the two other groups singing the song as a round, i.e. the second group joining in after the first has sung the first line. Now the small ostinato group are having the important role of supplying the accompaniment to the round and at the same time becoming more secure with their pitch by singing a limited number of notes.

The teacher might add one repetition of the round sung by small groups or solos to give confident singers an opportunity to shine.

The activity above takes into account the variety of musical abilities that may be met in a class but the idea of inclusion also embraces children with behavioural difficulties and music does have something to offer such children. All children get excited in music lessons and the organisation of the lesson needs to take account of this (see Chapter 8). However, children who have less of the inner checks and balances that enable them to comply with classroom rules can respond to an orderly music lesson so long as there are routines to follow. Having a well-structured lesson that follows a number of predictable patterns will help greatly. In Chapter 8 we will discuss signals for silence and for starting activities but also good beginnings and ends to lessons. The other aspect of music that helps many of such children is the opportunities for leadership that music-making in small groups offers. Attention-seeking children can have the need to assert themselves directed positively by being given a conducting role. Making provision for children's special needs is considered further in Chapter 8.

Also within the general understanding of the term inclusion there is understood to be the inclusiveness of a multi-faith and multi-cultural classroom, generally termed social inclusion. It can be said that music has an important role to play in reflecting not just the cultural traditions of the children within the particular school but also that of British society in general. Hence music plays its part in educating children about the variety of cultural backgrounds of British people but also extending their understanding beyond into other parts of the world. This will be explored further when looking at repertoire material for listening and singing and cross-curricular possibilities in Chapter 7.

The introduction of entitlement to modern foreign languages in the primary curriculum in 2010

This will be explored in greater depth in Chapter 7, but it is important to note here that singing is not just a way of enlivening the curriculum, i.e. an extrinsic motivation, but a specific strategy that supports key skills and concepts in language development. Many schools are collecting a range of songs or chants in their target languages.

Styles of learning

Successive ministers of education have expressed anxieties about levels of literacy and this has had the effect of focusing on spoken and written language, and of those two mostly the latter. Certainly the primary classroom is highly dependent on language but this needs to be compensated with opportunities for children to access skills and understanding through alternative modes. In support of this is the current interest in children's varied styles of learning and the importance of varying teaching strategies accordingly. The acronym VAK has become a useful reminder that as well as the auditory or verbal mode (A) there should be visual (V) aspects and the recognition that children need active or kinaesthetic (K) opportunities to stimulate those brain functions that are reached through physical engagement with a task. Please note that I resist the notion that children individually have particular modes of learning in favour of the idea that all children need a variety of forms of teaching and learning.

CASE STUDY

Ruth, a Year 4 undergraduate trainee teacher, was concerned about poor literacy skills in her Year 2 class. She decided to plan a session in which she read nursery rhymes to the class and let them listen to and enjoy the rhythm and rhyme in the songs. Then she directed the children to select specific instruments that they felt would sound appropriate to the action or words in the rhymes. For example, when reading 'Hickory Dickory Dock' together, the children chose a two-tone wood block to represent the 'tick tock', a slide of a beater up a glockenspiel to represent the mouse running up the clock, and a triangle 'ting' when the clock struck one.

REFLECTIVE TASK

Learning objective: To be able to recognise different learning styles in action.

Analyse the trainee teacher's activity above in terms of three teaching and learning styles, visual, auditory or kinaesthetic.

One aspect of the case study that may have struck you is that the teacher has taken into consideration that these are active young children but also that they will be more motivated if they are given opportunities to make choices for themselves. Moreover, the use of the instruments isn't just to add colour or 'fun' but emphasises the meaning of the words. Above all the children are 'kinaesthetically' involved.

Teaching music is highly reliant on gesture, both bodily and facial. Gesture conveys the pitch through hand movements up and down, the shape of a phrase through a lateral hand movement or the mood through the speed of gesture and facial expression. Conducting does all of these things, but above all maintains a sense of purpose, positive ethos and buoyancy during a music session. All of these are more significant than the words the teacher chooses to use.

PRACTICAL TASK PRACTICAL TASK PRACTICAL TASK PRACTICAL TASK PRACTICAL TASK

Learning objective: To understand further the distinctive nature of music.

Consider how you might teach something musical without using words and, if confident enough, carry it out with a willing colleague.

Why is music in the curriculum?

Finally, take a moment to be a little philosophical. The nature of music is difficult to pin down and yet we should try because we need to understand its place in the curriculum.

Music as a way of knowing

It has been argued that music is a form of language. One possible response could be that if music served the same purpose as spoken and written language, that of holding and expressing knowledge, then it would have no reason for being. Hence it should not be regarded as 'a way of knowing' in that precise sense. Philpott argues that, unlike language, music does not have a direct relation to objective phenomena in the world, it does not have a foundational link between sounds and the object of meaning (2001, p32). The other argument could be that both forms have many features in common, such as both having a grammar and an underlying structure. Cooke (1959) goes so far as to argue that particular forms of music communicate precise emotions. Between the two positions exists a hinterland in which there is a recognition that music is metaphorical and hence conveys meaning, it *logically resemble(s) certain dynamic patterns of human experience and has significant form in relation to the world of feelings: the meaning is implicit but not conventionally fixed* (Langer, 1942, p204).

Music as a school subject

Music has secured a place alongside other arts in the curriculum. Traditionally it has a place in the liberal arts that were seen to be of value regardless of their usefulness. Ken Robinson, a fierce advocate of the arts in education, wrote that:

> *Without the balance that an education in both the sciences and the arts can give, we should have, rather, a nation of beings with heads like computers, hands like robots and hearts like Caliban's* (1989, p25).

Despite the fact that if for some music holds a relatively low status in their lives or even, for cultural or religious reasons, none at all, for the majority it pervades their everyday activities by accompanying activities and is ubiquitous in the media. The question still remains as to whether education about and in music is necessary in a utilitarian sense or whether music is there as a function of life making experience at school richer. The *Music Manifesto Sing Up* website 'Continyou' begins by inclining towards the latter view.

> *Song can be used as a vibrant and positive start to the day through singing based breakfast clubs. After-school singing clubs and choirs can boost pupils' morale...*

It then goes on to tap into the extended school agenda by asserting that:

> *Song has the power to bring communities together and to engage with parents. It can also help us to identify with our own culture and to explore the culture and identity of others.*

However, it takes a more straightforwardly utilitarian line when it says that:

> *Singing is a valuable tool used to help children with speech and language difficulties improve their communication skills.* (2007)

In this book we have accepted all three principles with regard to singing and assumed their application to most other music activities. Ultimately we have assumed that for many of us, as Friedrich Nietzsche wrote, *without music life would be a mistake* (1889) and education is both preparation for, and part of, life.

What next? Looking to the future

The Core Standard requires newly qualified teachers (NQTs) *to maintain an up-to-date knowledge and understanding of:*

- *(C3) the professional duties of teachers and the statutory framework within which they work, and contribute to the development, implementation and evaluation of the policies and practice of their workplace...;*
- *(C10) a range of teaching, learning and behaviour management strategies and know how to use and adapt them...*

If you are less confident about your musical skills or knowledge and associated strategies, you can support *the policies and practice of the workplace* by demonstrating professional development and your ability to contribute with the skill that you do have. If you already have some musical skills and are able to contribute by playing an instrument or using your knowledge of particular genres of music, be innovative in the use of recorded music. The latter may join in or lead extra-curricular activities.

A SUMMARY OF **KEY POINTS**

> You need to 'audit' your own musical experience, skills and knowledge, so that you know where you are starting from in developing your music teaching abilities.

> The present English and Welsh music curricula can only be fully understood through knowledge of their history and contributors.

> The National Curriculum for music has four key activities and seven elements, most of which can be present in any one music lesson. However, each lesson will have particular focuses.

> Implementing the music curriculum requires resources which will found dispersed around a primary school.

> It is important to understand the contribution that the music curriculum may make to current initiatives.

REFERENCES REFERENCES **REFERENCES** REFERENCES **REFERENCES** REFERENCES

Cooke, D. (1959) *The language of music*. Oxford: Oxford University Press

Dalcroze, J. (1921/1967) *Rhythm, music and education* (trans. H.F.Rubinstein). Geneva: The Dalcroze Society

Damasio, A (2003) *Looking for Spinoza: Joy, sorrow and the feeling brain*. Orlando: Harcourt

DfES (2004) Every *Child Matters: change for children in schools*. Nottingham: DfES Publications

DfES and DCMS (2004) *The Music Manifesto*. Nottingham: DfES Publications

DfES (2006) *The Primary National Strategy*. Nottingham: DfES Publications

Langer, S. (1942) *Philosophy in a new key*. Cambridge MA: Harvard University Press

Nietzsche, F. (1889/1968) *Twighlight of the Gods*. London: Penguin

Orff, C. and Keetman, G.(1950) *Musik für Kinder*. Mainz: Schott.

QCA (1999) *The National Curriculum for England – music*. Norwich: HMSO

QCA (2004/5) *Music – Annual Report on curriculum and assessment*. Norwich: HMSO

Robinson, K. (ed.) (1989 reprint with additions) *The arts in schools*. London: Calouste Goulbenkian Foundation

Vygotsky, L. (1935/1978) *Mind in society: The development of higher psychological processes.* Cambridge MA: Harvard University Press

Walsh, M. (2003) *The Singing School initiative*. Manchester: Manchester Music Service

Websites

National Network of Arts in Health: www.nnah.org.uk

Music Manifesto National Singing Programme: www.singup.org link to www.continyou.org.uk/what_we_do/children_and_young_people/sing (accessed 1/1/2008)

2
Key musical skills – Listening and appraising

By the end of this chapter you should begin to understand and know about:

- the importance of listening both for yourself and for children;
- the implications of listening as described in the National Curriculum for music, e.g. listening with attention, listening for musical elements and effects and listening for how time and place influence musical style;
- planning for and implementing lessons to develop appraising skills.

This chapter addresses the following Professional Standards for QTS:
Q10, Q11, Q12, Q13, Q21, Q22

Introduction

PRACTICAL TASK PRACTICAL TASK PRACTICAL TASK PRACTICAL TASK PRACTICAL TASK

Learning objective: to analyse your own musical listening style.

Choose a song that is well known to you and listen in your most familiar format and circumstance. Now answer the following:

1. What format have you chosen and where is it being played?
   Consider the implications, both social and in terms of personal taste.

2. What is the genre of the music?
   What does this say about you?

3. How do you respond to the music?
   Do you hum along, tap foot or fingers? Do you let the sound float over you or do you listen out for particular moments?

If the form that you chose for the task was private rather than out loud, this may be because you were trying not to disturb anyone else, and music among your acquaintances and family is considered highly individual and is not generally a shared experience. If the music was shared it could be that you were deliberately trying to create an 'ambience' for others or you wanted the music as a background to a domestic task.

- Consider the extent to which this music is like the clothes you wear, an indication of the values you adopt and an indication of the style you are comfortable with or even aspire to. Is the music a form of comfort or have you chosen the challenge of the unfamiliar?
- Are you aware of the form of the song, where the chorus comes or when the end is approaching? Are there moments in the song where you listen particularly carefully?

You may find that you listen in different ways in different contexts. Some people find that they listen attentively when in a car. Others may listen while doing routine domestic jobs and enjoy the way the music can create a pleasurable ambience which masks the monotony of the task. You may also have found that at different moments in the music you listened with more or less attention. Generally listening in adult life is a leisure activity and we do not feel the need to listen out for detail such as recognising an instrument playing, and yet we may anticipate a particular melody and enjoy its return. This represents an analytical approach and appraisal in a form that makes the whole experience of listening more rewarding and therefore one that we want to encourage in children.

What is the difference between listening and appraising?

'Listening' is the term used in the National Curriculum for the specific skill of listening and the opportunity for applying knowledge and understanding about music.

The Programmes of Study Section 4 on listening requires pupils to be taught:

- to listen with attention to detail and to internalise and recall sounds with increasing aural memory;
- how the combined musical elements of pitch, duration, dynamics, tempo, timbre, texture and silence can be organised within musical structures and used to communicate different moods and effects;
- how music is produced in different ways and described through relevant established and invented notations;
- how time and place can influence the way music is created, performed and heard.

'Appraising' is the term used in the National Curriculum for evaluating music.

The Programmes of Study Section 3 on responding and reviewing – appraising skills, requires pupils to be taught to:

- analyse and compare sounds;
- explore and explain their own ideas and feelings about music using movement, dance, expressive language and musical vocabulary;
- improve their own and others' work in relation to its intended effects.

Hence appraising is the thinking and doing that results from listening. Within any arts education there needs to be thoughtful evaluation both during the work on the art product and summatively when the product is shared with others. This exercise of judgment is one of the key characteristics of the arts.

This chapter will look at the classroom strategies and associated issues first for listening and then appraising.

Listening

Why is listening important?

Listening is a cross-curricular skill. Without it children can miss a wide range of opportunities in the classroom. It is as if one whole sense is missing. However, in music activities it can be developed as a specific skill. The key musical listening moments are as follows.

1. Listening to instructions.
2. Listening for when to join in musical performance.
3. Listening to the rehearsing and performance of music for the need to make improvements.
4. Listening to performances to appraise the results.
5. Listening to recorded music to respond in some way.

PRACTICAL TASK PRACTICAL TASK PRACTICAL TASK PRACTICAL TASK PRACTICAL TASK

Learning objective: To learn about how children develop attentive listening.

When in your placement class work with a small group of children.

- The children are seated in a circle.

- Each has a hand-held percussion instrument.

- Direct them to make one single sound each in turn but only to start when the sound of the previous instrument has died away.

In this task we hope the children are exercising listening activities 1, 2 and 5 from the list above. But also this kind of listening is one that encourages social awareness and hence those aspects of music activity which support the broader curriculum as identified in Every Child Matters – both 'enjoy and achieve' and 'make a positive contribution'.

Possible barriers to listening

For children to listen with concentration there is a range of factors to be considered. The conditions of the classroom will contribute. Many classrooms are designed to be stimulating and these distractions may need to be reduced in some way. If there is no activity to focus on and the children are seated at tables at which they face each other, they will inevitably distract each other. They are not used to just listening without visual accompaniment. Additionally there may be special difficulties, such as:

- hearing problems;
- maintaining attention;
- emotional and behavioural disorders;
- tiredness.

The organisation and content of music lessons may be challenged by children with such conditions. However, do consider how this can be turned around and how in a music lesson such factors become more apparent and help lead to a diagnosis and helpful strategies. This is explored in more depth in Chapter 8.

Optimising listening

For simple listening to music the optimum condition might be lying on the floor looking at the ceiling. For this the school hall or a special space might be needed. If you know that children in your class could manage it, simply directing them to close their eyes is effective. However, often listening is accompanied by activity or linked visual experience. If children are listening to a performance they will have the sight of their own peers or other musicians playing instruments which provide extra cues as to which instruments are playing and when. This helps their appreciation of the structure and the textures of the music.

Listening to recorded music

Note: All references to specific pieces of music are listed in more detail in Appendix 5 with a variety of alternatives.

Listening to recorded music may seem to be a passive activity and hence something difficult for young and active children to manage. The purpose of this section is to make links with a range of other activities and hence to help to engage children with listening in an active manner.

Although the activity of listening is largely seen as integral to the activities of performing and composing, there is still one aspect which does not immediately appear to lie in this 'active' domain, and that is listening to recorded music. The choice of suitable recordings may be made with three principal criteria in mind.

1. The pieces should offer opportunities for active response by children.
2. They should clearly demonstrate musical points (musical elements).
3. There should be diversity of styles and genres.

Consider the value of developing adventurous tastes and open-mindedness in children at an early age. You need to be careful to help children to do this in ways which develop naturally from their previous experience of listening. You also need to adopt active approaches where possible in order to encourage attentive and thoughtful listening. Think about the range of possible styles and genres of music there are. Nothing is out of bounds unless the words in songs are likely to cause offence, but some forms are more effective than others.

Mood and story music for movement and writing to

Music for this purpose is best chosen for one of two characteristics:

- contrasting episodes;
- strong contrasts in, or the expression of, a general mood through, tempo, dynamics, texture and timbre.

Many pieces may have characteristics to which children can respond through movement. Some of the music may sound like background music to a film, changes in mood may suggest incidents in a story, various melodies may suggest characters. The teacher might stop the music at certain points and ask:

- what kind of character is this?
- what kind of place?
- what is the character doing?

The children can jot down notes about their responses. Then later these can be put together into a story.

PRACTICAL TASK PRACTICAL TASK PRACTICAL TASK PRACTICAL TASK PRACTICAL TASK

Learning objective: To develop an analytical listening ear.

This task is to encourage two different kinds of response: a kinaesthetic one and a reflective one both affective and cognitive.

Play a recording of 'Dawn' the first from the set of four *Sea Interludes* by Benjamin Britten.

Listen to the whole piece twice.

Use an A2 size paper to draw on with chalk – respond freely to the tempo (fast and slow), the pitch (up and downs) of the music.

Listen a second time and respond to these three questions:

1. What kind of a place does this represent for you?

2. What time of day?

3. Are there any people or animals in your place, if so who or what?

Did this activity (the kinaesthetic element) enable you to focus on the characteristics of the music? Specifically, were you aware of where there was a melody which rose and fell, whether instruments were alone or in combination and whether the music moved faster or slower or was louder or quieter (the cognitive element)? You may have become aware of the sense of space the music created with the long, simple unaccompanied melodies or the emotion expressed through loud climaxes or intense quietness (the affective element).

Having experienced this yourself, you will appreciate better how music may serve as a stimulus for expressive writing. Music can also create a strong sense of mood conducive to concentrated and well-focused work. With regard to music education, the children become more aware of characteristics in the music itself or at the very least the experience will have enabled them to become absorbed in the music and to have 'lost themselves' for some moments. This latter experience is significant and is an important aspect of response to the arts.

The following activity enables children to engage with the music in a similar way to the task you have just undertaken. This will have a drama or written outcome.

Teaching example

Journey into space

The teacher starts off by playing the recorded music *Thus Spake Zarathustra* by Richard Strauss, for a take-off. She pauses to ask the children what they see and how they feel. Then she moves on to play 'Neptune' from *The Planets* by Gustav Holst, which suggests travelling through space. She asks the children again the same questions.

Finally she directs the children to write about a space journey using the ideas that came to them when listening to the music.

Music for drawing and painting to

Children can often respond spontaneously to the rhythm, melody, and thin or dense textures of the music through 'taking a line for a walk' across the paper. The line or pattern can respond to the up-and-down contour of the melody or the jagged or smooth rhythm. Patterns can be suggested by the interweaving of instrumental parts in more complex textured music.

PRACTICAL TASK PRACTICAL TASK PRACTICAL TASK PRACTICAL TASK PRACTICAL TASK

Learning objective: To understand the connection between pattern in art and musical rhythm and melody.

Choose some recorded music that has a strong rhythmic character and with strong contrasts. 'Jupiter' from *The Planets* by Gustav Holst is a good example. Use a sheet of A2 paper and large chalks that will cover the paper quickly. While playing the music in the background, respond to the shape of the melody, tempo of the music and rhythmic shapes in a spontaneous way. Try to fill the paper with shapes and patterns.

Drawing to the music can be quite an analytical activity. The pattern of your line may show how well you have heard the character of the music. In such an exercise in school the children may show some appreciation of the music. However, many may respond quite simply to the mood of the music which can be a strong stimulus for imaginative work.

Music for joining in with

Adding a pulse or simple rhythm to music with a strong beat is one of the simplest ways of engaging with recorded or performed music. This might take the form of a variety of body sounds and could be associated with whole body movement or dance.

Teaching examples

Making use of rhythmic music (samba or traditional West African)

The children listen to the recorded music.

- If the class is a small group, the children might all have percussion instruments and join in spontaneously with the music.
- If the class is larger, the children listen to the music before joining in with instruments and see if they can identify rhythms.

The class is then split into groups. Within each group one child has an instrument and the others use body sounds. One group keeps a steady pulse while others follow the simple rhythms they have identified. The recorded music is started and then each group is brought in one at a time. At one point, the music is turned down so that the children are heard on their own.

Ambient music – music with interesting percussive sounds

The class are assigned, or choose for themselves, instruments or sounds. Then they follow the recorded music, listening for sounds like that of the instrument they hold. On hearing the music a second time they join in with their chosen sound when it is heard.

An example of this could be using the music *Rain Forest Dream by Joji Hirota*.

The children could use drums, triangles, chimes, wood blocks, and the focus would be on timbre.

Listening for musical elements

The National Curriculum for music is quite detailed about the aspects of music that pupils should be taught to recognise through their listening. They should be taught:

PoS 4b how the combined musical elements of: pitch, duration, dynamics, tempo, timbre, texture and silence can be organized within musical structures

and to explore and explain:

> *PoS 3 their own ideas and feelings about music using movement, dance, expressive language and musical vocabulary.*

It will be a good idea for you to collect examples of recorded music that illustrate musical elements particularly well.

Contemporary popular dance or disco music is good for background beat. But for awareness of dynamics, romantic orchestral music would be best. Music from the Baroque period is very good for clearly structured melodies, which is one reason why children particularly enjoy this and music of the Classical period. But best of all, children's awareness of the musical elements arises out of listening to their own compositions and performances.

Listening to music as a management strategy

Increasingly you will find recorded music being used in the background to lessons. Sometimes this has a very specific purpose associated with and prompting specific activities.

CLASSROOM STORY

Debbie, a Year 4 BA Primary Education trainee, always liked the idea of playing music in the classroom and decided to use this to help keep the classroom noise level down. She played a variety of genres of music each week because she wanted to find out which was the most effective. Initially the children responded well. She had the rule, 'if I cannot hear the music and you can't, then you are talking too loudly'. She started by playing panpipe music, to which the children did work quietly. But as she varied the styles she would often have to remind them of the rule and reinforce how she wanted them to work. Possibly the children became used to the music and no longer responded.

Another strategy she tried was to play music for the children to tidy up to. She introduced the *Mission Impossible* theme tune and instructed them that every time they heard the tune it meant they had to tidy up quickly and sensibly and be sitting on the carpet with their lips together and their legs crossed before the music finished. To start with, the children became overexcited and started to run around. So she turned off the music and explained that the behaviour was not acceptable. Throughout the following week the children became used to this form of tidying up; and responded better and it got to the stage when she did not have to tell them it was time to tidy up; they just did it as soon as they heard the music being played.

REFLECTIVE TASK

Learning objective: To evaluate whether music is seen as having value if used as background.

You may have your own view about whether using music as a management strategy is good use of music, or it may be that you consider it a good use of one genre and poor use of another. Consider how 'value' can be attached to such music by listening to it in other contexts.

Music genres

The importance of exposing children to a variety of musical types and styles is set out in the National Curriculum *PoS 5e*: *During the Key Stage, pupils should be taught the knowledge, skills and understanding through: a range of live and recorded music from different times and cultures*.

In general when choosing music I suggest you select primarily for its interest or attractiveness. The name is often irrelevant even if the music is to accompany a theme. For instance, Handel's *Water Music* doesn't sound at all like water. It would be much better to choose a piece called *Symphony no. 4* or *Music to Chill to* that happened to sound watery and not to mention the name. The experience of listening is more important than knowing the origins of the music.

I have found that instrumental music is better received than vocal music because vocal styles often sound amusing, exotic or simply odd to children and this distracts from the main purpose of the activity. However, in the case of popular styles there isn't usually a problem.

Examples of music from the history of Western art music

The National Curriculum *PoS 5e* draws attention to the need for: *a range of live and recorded music from different times...for example music by well known composers and performers*.

There are accepted conventions about the historical periods into which Western art music is divided.

Early or medieval and Renaissance (anything before seventeenth century)

Music characterised by distinctive instruments such as the lute and recorder, simple instrumental musical forms or choral music in which parts imitate like in a round such as:

- medieval dances;
- tudor dances;
- lute music.

The music is useful to add period atmosphere and accompaniments to dance.

Baroque (seventeenth and early eighteenth century)

Music that is more expressive and often very melodic but supported by distinctively independent accompanying parts. For example, *The Water Music* by George Frederick Handel; *Trumpet Voluntary* by Jeremiah Clark.

The music of this period will often have attractive melodies with a strong steady pulse.

Classical (later eighteenth century)

Often classical music includes dramatic contrasts and clear conventions including phrase or melody endings that are often predictable. For example, *Horn Concerto no.3* by Amadeus Mozart; *Dance of the blessed spirits* by Christobald Gluck.

You will find very attractive melodies and strong moods in the music.

Romantic (nineteenth century)

Music of the romantic period will usually be highly expressive and capable of arousing the emotions strongly. It is music that can convey a sense of narrative or drama. For example, *Pictures in an exhibition* by Mussorgsky has very varied moods; *Thus Spake Zarathustra* by Richard Strauss (music for the film *2001 A Space Odyssey*) has dramatic fanfare-like music.

Modern (early and middle twentieth century)

The music of this period is often experimental and sometimes difficult to listen to but some styles have become accepted in advertising and film scores. Some music takes on the characteristics of popular music and can be very accessible. For example, *Appalachian Spring (variations on a shaker hymn)* by Aaron Copeland has an excellent tune, and atmospheric music; *Sea Interludes* from the opera *Peter Grimes* by Benjamin Britten has very distinct layers of sound with clear instrumentation and strong mood.

Contemporary (late twentieth and twenty-first century)

In this period there is a return to music that is more accessible. Styles include fusions with popular and world musics and extended phrases based on repetitions or simple components. For example, *Fearful Symmetries or The Chairman Dances* by John Adams is highly energetic, dance-like music; *Drumming* by Steve Reich.

World musics

This is the term used to describe music from non-Western music traditions. Some commentators disagree with the term because they don't find this binary distinction helpful. Most music traditions have their popular and classical aspects and this might be a more useful distinction that reflects the reality of the music.

There is some worth in actively creating the ambience of a place through its music. The gongs and metallophones of Indonesian gamelan music have a very distinctive timbre. The ambience of the piece may suggest a characteristic of the place. Traditional music from China relies greatly on the play of timbres from one instrument to another and is often impressionistic or suggestive of atmosphere. North Indian music is also atmospheric and may be technically very complex. It is also worth using examples in purely musical contexts so that they lose their 'exotic' connotations that they may otherwise take on if associated with geographical locations.

Examples include the following.

- African drumming (African traditional music from Ghana): unpitched drums (but in broad pitch bands) play complex rhythms (polyrhythms) that interrelate but are distinctive.
- Indonesian gamelan: music created by an orchestra of gongs, metallophones and drums. For each section of the music the instrumentalists each play repeated phrases all of which interrelate in interesting ways.
- North Indian classical music: atmospheric music often associated with time of day.
- Indian popular music: Bhangra or Hindi film music: recognisably Indian but with familiar touches of Western influence.
- Irish traditional dance: emphasis on clear melodies and strong beat.

Music from different cultures will have distinctive or unusual instruments and unfamiliar ways of playing such instruments. If the music is a dance, a comparison can be made with contemporary or British popular dance music familiar to the children. In the case of a song, the way the melody is decorated by the singer will vary greatly from one tradition to another. The music may be constructed in different ways and have different performing traditions. Indonesian gamelan music is carefully planned so that each of the several players has a distinctive part that interweaves with others.

Popular music

Although children will have heard plenty of popular music the range of styles may be quite narrow. It is worth including non-chart music which will have an appeal for children. Choose pieces with clarity of beat or rhythm, clarity and simplicity of melody, or with intriguing 'effects'. The definition of the category 'popular' is increasingly difficult these days but however ill-defined, it is well worth exploiting. With children at Key Stages 1 or 2, music that has some classic status to it, and hence is a little in the past, will often be a better choice. Music of the 1960s goes down very well, particularly music of the Beatles.

CLASSROOM STORY

Debbie, a Year 4 BA student, decided to try playing popular music to control classroom noise level. She was worried at first because she expected the children to become overexcited. However, surprisingly it had the opposite effect. The children did 'chatter' a little when it first came on but she told them that if they talked too much the music would be turned off. She then slowly began to notice that the children were quietly getting on with their work and actually humming along to the music. She allowed this to happen as long as they completed their work.

RESEARCH SUMMARY RESEARCH SUMMARY RESEARCH SUMMARY RESEARCH SUMMARY

Lucy Green explores the use of popular music in the classroom.

On the one hand she writes:

Popular music has often been cast in antipathy to education, a classic expression of which is Pink Floyd's hit, 'Brick in the Wall', which reached Number 1 in the British charts in 1982. The song puts anti-educational sentiments ('We don't need no education') into the mouths of a chorus of children, suggests that schools engage in 'thought control' and implies that teachers bully children. It sustained some criticism at the time, and many teachers felt that it was damaging... problems arise because pupils can be divided amongst themselves over popular music, narrow and partisan in their tastes, and over-influenced by the charts, especially when younger (2001, pp159–160).

She points out that there are worries about the analytical approach to pop music at secondary school level from pop musicians themselves in case, as musicians would say, it loses its soul or the enjoyment is killed. However, these musicians looked back favourably at any positive experience of pop music in school whether through making music or listening.

Semi-popular genres: film music and musicals

Film music is a very popular genre and the music will often be familiar to the children. In a song such a 'Halleluia' used in the film *Shrek* the children will enjoy joining in the chorus even if the rest of the words are obscure. Scores such as *Star Wars* are highly dramatic and can accompany acting out stories effectively. Classic scores such as *Spartacus* and *The Mission* are popular with youth orchestras because of their emotive and strong melodic lines. Film music is intended to be atmospheric and to enhance mood or action and hence can be very effective as a stimulus for art work or writing.

Listening to live performance

An important but occasional aspect of music education is listening to live performances. This is significant from the Early Years onward. Youth Music and Northumbria University (2006) research on the impact of musical activities on the development of pre-school children has recognised that regular contact with musicians has a positive impact on communication, language and mathematical skills, and on emotional, social, physical and cultural development. The *Music Manifesto* no. 2 (DfES, 2006) then goes on to propose that: *training programmes be extended and developed for musicians wishing to work in early years settings*. In recent years the funding for creative partnerships has enabled a range of professional musicians to work in schools. The *Manifesto* proposes that such arrangements should not be subject to the vagaries of occasional funding but become embedded as entitlements for children. Hence there is a recognition that development in the arts is 'caught' from role models and vivid direct experience, both of which are very significant in giving children the appetite and persistence to succeed.

Such experiences are quite varied but one important factor is the participation of children in the performances.

CLASSROOM STORIES

Two orchestral musicians worked with two primary classes in the Lowry Theatre art gallery to develop instrumental compositions based on pictures in the gallery. As part of this experience the musicians played their own instruments in a variety of ways to encourage the children to be creative with their own instruments. Then these group compositions were rehearsed back at school and in the following week were performed as part of the two musicians' orchestral concert performance by the Northern Chamber Orchestra of *Pictures at an Exhibition* by Moussorgsky. The inclusion of the children in the concert drew the parents into a shared experience that was new for most and hence gave even more weight to the experience for the children.

In his book *World musics in education*, Malcolm Floyd (2006) describes a project of the Ghanaian group Dagarti Arts with Frogmore Community School and associated primary schools. In this case the children were taught some of the music that the group had performed, simple drum polyrhythms, clapping rhythms and call-and-response songs. Here the children begin as audience and then become part of the performing group. This participatory format recognises that children are less content to remain as passive listeners even with a strong visual element to the performance. It also recognises that the children learn more through first-hand experience.

REFLECTIVE TASK
REFLECTIVE TASK

Learning objective: To understand more about the nature of musical knowledge.

The National Curriculum requires that at Key Stage 2 children should be taught *how time and place can influence the way music is created, performed and heard*. Consider how children might recognise that music comes from a particular time or place.

Then read the Research Summary below.

Recognise that there is a cautionary message here. Consider the nature of musical knowledge and what is useful for children and what could get in the way of their experience of music.

Swanwick (1994) uses the terms 'knowledge about music' and 'knowledge of music'. He advocates the emphasis on children's acquisition of knowledge of music or knowledge of how (practical skills) rather than knowledge about music (contextual knowledge).

RESEARCH SUMMARY RESEARCH SUMMARY **RESEARCH SUMMARY** RESEARCH SUMMARY

Keith Swanwick notes *that knowledge about things can so easily be acquired in non-musical ways* (1994, p15).

In *Teaching music musically* (1996) he emphasises further the importance of experiencing music directly by first hand. He argues that music lessons should not become yet another opportunity to learn about a subject expressed in language and mediated through language. He goes on to argue that music should be experienced and should be the medium through which any musical understanding is acquired. Thus he sees music as the medium as well as the message.

Swanwick's message is a useful one to carry with you as you plan music lessons so that the children have the maximum opportunity to engage in practical music. However, the companion activity to *listening* is *appraising* and this inevitably requires talk. But this talk enriches the experience of listening to music.

Appraising

Appraising happens informally while children are composing music or rehearsing performances. But it may happen formally in a plenary guided by the teacher. In formal situations the teacher models appraising or guides the children in the skill of appraising with key questions.

CLASSROOM STORY

A class of children has been formed into pairs and each of the children in the pair hold contrasting instruments. The children have created short musical 'conversations'. The teacher has given the children the preliminary tasks of echoing each other and then contrasting each other. Then they have all had some time to create their own pieces using either method. Some pairs are invited to perform to the rest of the group. Members of the group are invited to comment on aspects of one composition with questions such as:

Do A and B copy each other or contrast/do the opposite of each other?

She might then introduce an extra element that she detected in the performance by asking:

When was their musical conversation loud and when was it quiet?

REFLECTIVE TASK
REFLECTIVE TASK

Learning objective: To develop analysis of teachers' questioning.

- Consider how the teacher constructs questions to prevent children from answering only 'yes' or 'no'.
- Consider the extent to which being able to see the performers helps children to respond to the questions.

By appraising, the children are in effect peer or self-assessing in the same way that they are encouraged to do across the curriculum under the banner of 'assessment for learning'. In the arts this form of assessment has always been an essential component; without it there can be no creativity. The creativity in refining a performance or composition must necessarily involve making judgements and choices.

CASE STUDY

A teacher has led a class of children learning the round 'Have you seen the ghost of John?'

The children are quite confident in singing the song all together. The teacher recites just the words, to focus the children's attention on these only, and then asks the children to think about the tempo of the song bearing in mind its mood and character. The children discuss in pairs and she asks for feedback. One child answers that the song is funny so it should be sung in a lively way. Another answers that it is a gloomy subject and would be even funnier if sung slowly. The teacher moves on to thinking about dynamics and the children consider whether the song should be loud or quiet or maybe a bit of both to create surprises.

The teacher is involving the children in the process of making a performance more expressive and engaging to listen to. She leads but involves the children all the way along.

More informal appraisal opportunities take place when children are working independently. It could be that the children have to decide which instrument would be best suited to accompany the spoken words, *Gold and money* or *the mousie's run away with it* from the rhyme 'Burnie's Hill' (see Chapter 8). They may be offered a limited choice by the teacher to prevent lengthy discussions and trials but the children test the instruments quietly for their *chinking* or *scampering* quality.

Then later in this activity a pair of children who have the 'mousie' words decide which instrument is to begin the music or the manner in which they are to be played. This is the most productive appraisal for children when they have had plenty of experience.

Be prepared for the children to need to acquire the skills. To begin with they may judge on the basis of the biggest or loudest instrument regardless of the task. But with some good strong positive encouragement for those who do exercise careful judgement, the others will begin to pick up the message.

Teaching example

A class of children is divided into groups of five. The children within each group are numbered 1, 2, 3, 4 and 5. Each member of the group has decided on a body sound they are going to make but also takes a turn at leading the rest of the group. To begin with, 5 directs the group by pointing to one of the others at which they make their sound and the others are directed in succession in a recognisable pattern. Having completed the composition, number 5 decides he wants to have a better ending so he tells the group to repeat the final sound. They try this but the leader does not like the effect so they try sounding all together. The leader thinks this is better so they have a second go at performing the composition.

When appraising live performance, children can describe more accurately what they have heard and description is the most important aspect of appraising. It is worth remembering that for younger children in particular a multi-sensory approach enriches the learning experience. Hence a parallel visual experience with hearing will have more impact.

Teacher appraisal

You, as the teacher, will also be appraising children's performance through listening and will be identifying a small sample of children (perhaps three or four) to observe more carefully and about whom to make records to inform future activities. See more about this in Chapter 8 under assessment.

A SUMMARY OF **KEY POINTS**

> Everyone has favourite ways of listening and favourite types of music. We can reflect this in the way we introduce listening to music for children.

> Listening is an important cross-curricular skill and music has an important role in helping children to develop this skill.

> There is a range of barriers to listening. The conditions or variety of opportunities for listening will help to overcome these.

> Listening to recorded music can be woven into the school day in a number of ways, but it is also part of set music lessons. For children, listening to their own compositions and performances are important opportunities.

> Listening to recorded music should be thought of as an active process. The mind is active when listening to features of the music and children should be encouraged to think actively by doing activities in response to music.

> The choice of music to listen to should reflect a wide range of styles and genres from different times and places.

> Appraising is the name given to the thinking part of the listening process. Most significantly this relates to the continuous making of judgments in the composing or performing process.

What next?

The Core Standard C15 requires teachers to:

> *Have a secure knowledge and understanding of the subjects/curriculum areas they teach including: the contribution that their subjects/curriculum areas can make to cross-curricula learning, recent relevant developments, and related pedagogy.*

The funding under the heading 'creative partnerships' has in the past and will continue to fund innovative projects that promote the work of artists in schools in line with the proposals set out in the DfES and DCMS document *All Our Futures* (1995) and the *Music Manifesto*. Consider what a performing musician could contribute to a project that you have in mind for your future work (or recent past) in school if the funding were available.

REFERENCES REFERENCES **REFERENCES** REFERENCES **REFERENCES** REFERENCES

DfES and DCMS (2004) *The Music Manifesto*. Nottingham: DfES Publications

Floyd, M. (2006) *World musics in education*. London: Scholar Press

Green, L. (2001) *How popular musicians learn: A way ahead for music education*. Aldershot: Ashgate.

Swanwick, K. (1994) *Musical knowledge – Intuition, analysis and musical education*. London: Routledge

Swanwick, K. (1996) *Teaching music musically*. London: Routledge

Youth Music (2006) *Turning their ears on*. In *The Music Manifesto* no. 2 (DfES 2006). DfES Publications

3
Key musical skills – Performing using the voice

By the end of this chapter you will begin to understand and know about:

- **the importance of vocalising and singing both for yourself and for pupils;**
- **the place of singing as an ongoing skill described in the National Curriculum for music;**
- **how to plan for and implement opportunities to develop singing skills.**

This chapter addresses the following Professional Standards for QTS:
Q1, Q2, Q4, Q5, Q7(a), Q10, Q14, Q15, Q17, Q18, Q19, Q22, Q23, Q25(a,b,c,d), Q27, Q28, Q30

Introduction

The first section of the Music National Curriculum is about performance. This is what most of us associate with musical activity. If we were to say *Jane is a musician*, people will assume Jane is a singer or plays an instrument. We do know that she could be a conductor or a composer but the actual production of music is the primary activity. This chapter looks at how you can develop children's performance skills and the necessary skills for yourself to do this confidently. We introduce you to the variety of vocal sounds, body sounds and instruments and how these can be combined to make interesting textures of sound.

At its most simple, performing is acquiring the skill to be able to control sounds. Children need to have many opportunities to gain these control skills so that they are able to have an ever-extending repertoire of sounds at their disposal, giving them the raw materials by which they can engage in music-making and make music of their own. Children will have different levels of skill, depending on their prior experience and the opportunities which they have had to handle the specific sound-maker or instrument.

A helpful guide when considering a hierarchy of differing levels of skill might be broadly defined as: with competence, with confidence, with accuracy or *I can make the sound, I can happily and confidently make the sound, I can make all sorts of sounds depending on the sounds I need or want!*.

Vocal skills

Singing is one such performing skill and the voice a dynamic sound-maker, as this Zimbabwean proverb captures.

If you can walk you can dance
If you can talk you can sing

Just as you are somewhere on the musical map, you are also somewhere in the vocal vortex. We all have a perception of ourselves in terms of this very personal and intimate skill; our voices are literally part of us, fundamental to the way we communicate with each other and how we express who we are. We are each sensitive to the ways our unique voice is perceived by others.

The ability to vocalise is a precious skill. Human voices are richly varied in their tone and timbre, each is individual and highly personal. So distinctive is the voice of a mother that a child can recognise this sound within days of being born. The voice is a versatile sound-maker with infinite variations which can be adapted to meet every human situation, to soothe, to warn, to cherish, to coax. Voices whisper, speak, exclaim, proclaim, shout, shriek, scream, sigh, laugh – and they also hum, doodle and sing.

PRACTICAL TASK PRACTICAL TASK PRACTICAL TASK PRACTICAL TASK PRACTICAL TASK

Learning objectives:

• To listen with a purpose to the rich variety of ways in which people use their voices to convey meaning and emotions to others.

• To appraise the means by which this is communicated.

Take three different contexts to notice those around you communicating through speech; e.g. a conversation with a group of friends, a teacher talking with an individual pupil, a conversation overheard on a bus, an adult speaking to a baby, children communicating in a playground.

Listen carefully for a minute or so. As close as possible to the event, jot down as many different ways in which the individuals manipulated and controlled their voices to express emotions or meaning as you can.

Do you notice any patterns? How does it seem to work? Did you hear changes in volume, tone, pace, pitch, timbre and inflections in their speech? Can you hear the musical elements coming into play?

It is no accident that the first practical task in a section on vocal skills begins, not with a vocal activity, but with a listening activity. If you could have witnessed your own emerging language-acquisition skills as a baby you would notice that this begins with hearing, perceiving sounds. At first sounds have no meaning but, as babies very quickly begin to recognise through their relationships with and reactions from and with others, the vocal sounds that human beings make provoke actions and behaviours in those around them. These special sounds capture attention. As the child begins instinctively to recognise that there is a relationship between vocal sounds and actions, then the hearing takes on a significance, a purpose and shift to the more acute skill of listening. Listening is the foundation of successful vocalising and singing.

The child as young as three months will begin to play independently with their own vocal equipment to try to create their own sounds. They take physical pleasure in the sensation. These early sounds are often quickly rewarded by the positive attention of a parent or carer who, in the optimum conditions, will encourage this fledgling vocal skill by repeating back the sound, playing with the sounds themselves, joining in with a playful vocal conversation. The natural process appears to be perception then production.

Of all the instruments that might be found in the primary classroom the voice is the most portable, potentially the most flexible and it doesn't cost a penny. Any surprising moment or unplanned opportunity that suddenly seems to present itself to a musical interpretation can employ this fascinating instrument in an instant.

CLASSROOM STORY
The bee – capitalising on opportunities for vocalising

Cassie was ten minutes into a dance lesson with her Year 2 class in the hall. The children had warmed up. As she began to give the children their next instruction, Cassie noticed that the children at the back of the hall were distracted, there was agitated movement, the children were making a range of anxious, surprised, curious or in some cases frightened vocal sounds. There was a bee in the hall, it had come in through the open window on this sunny afternoon. As a distracting strategy Cassie asked the children to make the buzzing sound of the bee and to move to a more distanced space from the offending insect using the same flying motions and movements as the bee was using. The children were much more engaged in this novel activity, the bee became a positive focus, the children extended their vocal range and the bee, left unmolested, flew back out of the window. The next day, Cassie brought in a bee puppet. The children played with their buzzing voices, buzzing really high and low, swooping between pitches following the contours of the puppet bee's flight. There were individual bee singers and a whole-class swarm. The final stage was the children using voices and finger play to join in with the different pitch contours that they heard in a recording of 'The flight of the bumble bee' by Rimsky-Korsakov. Cassie also revived the little singing game that the children had learned in Reception.

♪ ♪ ♪♪♪ ♪♪
                             e
                                c

Hi-cke-ty pi-cke-ty bum-ble bee,

♪ ♪ ♪ ♪ ♪
                             e
                                c

Can you sing your name for me?

♪ ♪♪♪ ♪
                        e
                           c

Lu-cy Lo-ckett is my name

Having the skill and confidence to use the voice in an extensive range of expressive ways is a vital tool for every teacher seeking to build a repertoire of strategies to inspire, engage, encourage and motivate children in their learning. Effective teachers use their voices with incredible skill and a great deal of confidence, but they had to start somewhere. You can probably notice how you use your voice much more effectively to gain and hold children's attention as you have had more opportunities to listen to others, to hear yourself and to practise different techniques and have guidance and encouragement from your class teachers. This is the beauty of a skill: the more you use it the better it gets.

The responses, comments and views of others can sensitise us to the qualities and effectiveness of our vocal skills which can be recognised, encouraged and celebrated or at best ignored, at worst belittled.

Individuals are often much more critical in their perception of their own level of competence than is actually the case. So let's take a reality check.

PRACTICAL TASK PRACTICAL TASK PRACTICAL TASK PRACTICAL TASK PRACTICAL TASK

Learning objective: Physically to produce a variety of vocal sounds and explicitly analyse the characteristic features that express meaning.

Find a spare five minutes in a place on your own.

Read and say the phrases below aloud with as much expression as you can muster.

It's important that you actually vocalise the words, not just imagine saying them. This is so that you can feel them, hear them and notice the physical sensation.

If the words conjure up an aural memory or image go with it.

I love you!	That was brilliant!	Watch out!	This is hard!	Are we there yet?
Nearly there!	You'll never do it!	I won't, won't, won't!		
I'm sorry!	Can we, should we?	Come on down!	Am I bovvered!	
Suits you, sir!	You've won a million pounds!	Mmmmmm!		
You are the weakest link. Goodbye!				

How did you use your vocal skills?

What was it about the way you used your voice which communicated your feelings, meaning or intentions?

Was it the dynamics of your voice, be it quiet, soft, hushed, muted or stressing words, raising the volume suddenly, shouting for full effect?

Perhaps you used the pitch of your voice. Did your voice get higher and higher as you became more angry or more excited? Did you use a sing-song quality to cajole, to sooth or to taunt?

Play around with your skill by changing the way you say the words. Can you change the meaning? You should be consciously noticing now how the expressive qualities of the musical elements can work. Are you gaining confidence? Have you gained greater control of your voice by noticing and practising, listening and appraising or perceiving and producing?

REFLECTIVE TASK

Learning objective: To create a realistic audit of your current personal vocal skills:

This quiz is all about you in the places and spaces that you inhabit with the people you know and meet and the events and circumstances, that make up your daily life.

Before you read the statements, take a few minutes to picture yourself putting your voice into action at different times and in different environments over the past day or so at home, in university, in school, on your own, with friends, with children, in the car, in a pub or club, on holiday, at a family, cultural or religious ceremony, etc.

People's perceptions of their vocal skills are often more limited than they actually are. Where do you place yourself in this range of statements? Circle the number that fits best.

Don't worry about how well you think you use your voice, just if and when you do.

	Always	Often	Sometimes	Never
I use my voice expressively to tell stories	1	2	3	4
I use my voice to express pleasure or give praise	1	2	3	4
I use my voice to gain or hold attention	1	2	3	4

I use my voice to show interest in or concern for others 1	2	3	4
I use my voice to express excitement or achievement 1	2	3	4
I use my voice to convey anger, disappointment or disdain 1	2	3	4
I sing along to music when I'm alone 1	2	3	4
I sing along to music with others 1	2	3	4
I sing with my children 1	2	3	4
I sing with my family 1	2	3	4
I sing with my friends 1	2	3	4
I sing with others in private 1	2	3	4
I sing with others in public 1	2	3	4
I sing on my own with children 1	2	3	4
I sing on my own with adults 1	2	3	4

I wonder how you would analyse your responses? It is probable that you had many 1s and 2s for the first section, but the second section, which specifically refers to singing, may have had a different complexion to it.

Most individuals are quite happy to hum or sing on their own in private but not in public. Some teachers would be anxious singing in front of their peers but quite happy to do so with children. As social beings we might comfortably join in with others singing happy birthday to a friend while not wanting to be singled out to sing solo. Our singing confidence changes depending on the circumstances.

In addition, there appears to be quite a jump between the use of the voice and the singing section. This is the area that can most fruitfully bear rewards in developing both yours and, in turn, children's vocal confidence and competence.

As the success in developing a skill relies on repetition and practice for consolidation and extension, so the quality and type of experiences which we have and our emotional and intellectual responses will be important. If the process is positive and enjoyable, receiving praise and encouraging reinforcement we will be motivated to repeat the experience. Negative or dismissive responses will inhibit the desire to repeat the experience, interfering with both the willingness and confidence to try again and thus use and develop that skill.

The attitude of the teacher, or significant other, will be important. Giving encouragement, looking for developments, recognising and affirming what the child can already do is an important feature of facilitating learning.

If babies instinctively learn through vocal play and practice, perhaps this is an important feature of scaffolding for gaining vocal confidence (Vygotsky, 1935). Voice play could be viewed as the child's early, independent, creative improvisation and a helpful foundation for potential singers of all ages.

CLASSROOM STORY

Changing our singing perceptions

Debs had decided to take music as a specialism in Year 3 of her BA course because she had enjoyed her university music sessions in Years 1 and 2. She had realised that although she didn't play an instrument she had plenty of skills to share with her pupils. Although she had not initially felt that she was a singer, Debs realised that as an individual and as a teacher she had a great deal of expertise in using her voice in all sorts of expressive ways. Voice play gave Debs a way in to being more confident in using her singing voice in front of her peers and with her classes in school. She felt quite confident in modelling and adding vocal sound effects to stories, inciting children to swoop their voices to help the rocket lift off, to recreate two-note siren sounds to represent the fire engine as a stimulus for role play for Bonfire Night Safety. Having played along with her voice, singing a short song with the children no longer seemed so daunting. Once she crossed that psychological *can't do* barrier and turned it into a *can do* she didn't look back.

Creating a singing classroom

Find out where you already are

Learning in any area involves recognising where you are already. We each learn through being challenged by new experiences and sensations and matching this to our existing knowledge and understanding or skill. If the match is too great we give up as the learning seems outside our scope. If the match is too small we tread water and eventually become bored. Successful learning often begins with a gradual movement from the known and familiar, within our comfort zone, toward the new and unfamiliar.

In the previous section you have been finding out where you are in the 'vocal vortex'. The same needs to be considered for your pupils.

In home, community and school settings children will have had a wide range of different vocal and singing experiences. Many will be familiar with and join in with rhymes and simple songs learned from family members, TV or radio programmes or favourite audio CDs. The chants and songs with which children are familiar may vary from one language or cultural tradition to another. Some children will have had enjoyable, regular opportunities to use their voices and sing with adults; others may not. Some children will be very confident in using their voices individually but not with a group or vice versa, while others will be reluctant, hesitant or even fearful.

Model a positive attitude

James Wild, a founder member of the Sing for Pleasure organisation, suggested that enthusiasm for singing is caught, like measles. A first step for creating a singing classroom is for you to generate your enthusiasm and let it become contagious. Your actions can show that singing is a fun thing to do. If you are concerned to create a positive and supportive environment for children to feel safe to explore and take risks with their voices then you need to reflect this in your attitude and behaviour. It is more important that you build an active, participatory, shared sense of vocal playfulness and fun with children than you sing with the perfect voice. In nurturing positive attitudes toward singing you are laying the foundations for your children's openness to a form of human expression which is fundamental.

If vocal play and using your voice in all sorts of ways is something that is part of your teaching repertoire then it also becomes part of the children's learning repertoire. Look for opportunities to push the boundaries of your own use of the spoken and singing voice.

Shared learning experiences can often be very rewarding, a shared journey can provide new opportunities and open up communal experiences. If the children see their teacher trying out and improvising vocal sounds they are more likely to see this as a good thing to do. If vocal confidence and motivation are good for children then it's good for teachers. It is also important that all contributions are valued, so be ready for the unexpected. Sometimes untimely individual hums, howls, oos or ahs may occur if a child cannot think of a sound initially but suddenly thinks of a fabulous voice sound later. Consider how you will ensure that the smallest participation and experiment is thoughtfully and sensitively received.

PRACTICAL TASK PRACTICAL TASK PRACTICAL TASK PRACTICAL TASK PRACTICAL TASK

Learning objective: To closely observe, record, audit and contribute to the use of voice play and singing in the school context.

On your next visit to school take time to notice children, teachers and other adults using voice play and singing in the nursery, the classroom, at assembly and on the playground.

Are there times when the children sing to themselves? Young children will often sing doodle as they are engaged in other tasks. Is this happening? What response do the children get from their teacher, from you or from others? Do children use their voices differently in the playground and with their friends than in class? Are you surprised by anyone?

Talk to the class teacher about the songs the children already know. Find ways of learning these songs yourself. Ask the children to sing their songs for you and with you. Create a singing audit for your class. Make up a song box of songs that the children know and like. Look for opportunities to use singing in your everyday teaching.

Starting points and strategies

Stories
Many stories include environmental or other sounds as part of the content. Use your voice to create the sounds and ask the children to join in, suggesting their own ideas. All stories involve characters. You will instinctively be using your voice to create characters so that the children can recognise them. Think about how you can make this more conscious and obvious. The Three Bears have significantly different voices: the low growly dad, the middle melodious mum, the high squeaky baby. The Three Billy Goats Gruff come in three sizes; show this in your voice. Children enjoy participating in repeated dialogue so they will quickly mimic the special voices you are modelling. As you listen to the children's versions, notice how high their squeaky voices are and how low their growly voice is. It is likely that their individual high and low voices will vary in range.

Poems and chants
Rhythmic, unison speaking adds another dimension to the speaking voice and is an effective way for us all to become familiar with and more comfortable with our vocal equipment. Gaining control over the instrument, making it quiet, loud, getting louder, getting quieter, is all part of the process. Speeding up and slowing down can add colour and expression to chanting or rapping which is yet another form of voice control. Inviting individual, pairs or small groups of children to say a particular part can provide

spaces for their creative ideas and performance hence fostering more individualised learning.

Breaking out

Finding the singing voice and distinguishing it from the speaking voice is an important step in development. Although the singing voice uses some of the same characteristics as the spoken voice, there is more emphasised use of pitch and duration. As soon as we need to sustain the sound to shift from speaking to singing we also need to give a little more breath.

PRACTICAL TASK PRACTICAL TASK PRACTICAL TASK PRACTICAL TASK PRACTICAL TASK

Perhaps we can think of the singing voice as sounds with a sigh or a hum. Give it a try. Make the sound 'Moo'. Try it a few different ways. When you are ready, make the 'oo' sound last a bit longer each time. Did you notice you need more breath? Try keeping the 'oo' sound going on its own. You are singing.

Breaking out is using a variety of sounds that sit between the speaking and singing voice; they require more breath to sustain and are a short step from singing, they can also help us to feel the sensation of using different pitches in our vocal range outside the usual speaking range. Think about animal sounds, machine sounds, airport sounds, playground sounds, traffic sounds – the list is endless.

CLASSROOM STORY
Omar breaks out. Giving children the chance to find their voice

Rachel had sung lots of simple action songs with her Year 1 class. She found out from the teacher and the children which songs they knew, and had observed the children singing in class and in assembly. These were the songs she began with. While she sang with and listened to the children singing she noticed that there was one child, Omar, who joined in with gusto and confidence but whose voice always sounded much lower than the other children. When listening to the children speaking she noticed that Omar's speaking voice was also quite low. Quite by chance she had used an action rhyme with the children to complement the story that the children were reading, which involved a steam train.

Up like a rocket
Down like the rain
Round and round
Like a railway train

The children said the chant, stretched up or down to the positional words and marched around to the last line. Instinctively, Rachel, added at the end *and here are our train sounds*. The children were choo-chooing as they moved. Some children began to hiss the steam and some hooted, just like a train whistle. Omar, who had always used his low, chest voice, tried a hoot and unexpectedly finding his head voice, seemed quite amazed by the sound. He continued to repeat the sound, playing with it, checking out that he could still find it when he wanted. He was beaming from ear to ear. It was a new physical sensation for him. During the following week, Rachel noticed that Omar was using his new sound to himself very quietly during choosing time, he also used both it and the actions with his friends in the playground. A new sensation and a breakthrough in vocal control!

Getting ready for song

PRACTICAL TASK PRACTICAL TASK PRACTICAL TASK PRACTICAL TASK PRACTICAL TASK

Learning objective: To prepare your own voice for singing in order to teach children to prepare theirs.

Singing is a physical activity and warming up the body and voice before embarking on more focused voice work is an important helping mechanism. If we are stiff and anxious our voices become stiff and anxious too: they tighten up. Loosening up the danger spots of tension – the knee joints, shoulder muscles, neck muscles, jaw and mouth – can all have beneficial effects. Make it fun and enjoy the physical exercise. If a laugh comes, enjoy that vocal experience too.

Try swinging arms backwards and forwards, loosen up and bend the knees as you go. Try skiing. Hunch shoulders to ears and hold tensely for three seconds then relax and let go. Roll the head gently forward onto the chin, slowly move to the left, back to the centre, then to the right and finally gently come back to the starting position. Relax the jaw with some very sticky toffee-chewing motions.

Make an echo game of some of your voice play sounds, use finger play and actions to reflect the characteristics or qualities of the sound and get the children to lead.

Make up an echo chant using current catch phrases that have different pitches or use lines from recently read stories or poems.

Before sneaking into singing, practise creating some extra breath for the song to sit on. Blow out all of the breath that you can and let the breath rush back in. Try it again but this time let the breath back in more slowly, filling up your lung balloon. Practise some controlled breathing out by imagining a candle in front of your mouth and let the breath out slowly and gently so that the candle doesn't blow out.

Small songs

Songs do not have to have lots of notes. Having sung conversations with children using just one note can be a start. A question-and-answer structure is a useful tool. Your sung question could be for the whole class, particular groups or named individuals. Greetings, days of the week, class routines are all useful sources of improvised repertoire. Expect a variety of answers, chanted, sung on your note or sung on different notes. Look for children eager to sing back on their own. If singing individually, encourage children to respond in whatever way they want. They could copy your one note, use one of their own or something entirely different. Try it and see. Taking the register using different voices has the potential for tiny individual vocal responses. I have often been surprised by the responses of students with this activity. Having stated that I am going to sing their name, just on one note, but that they can respond in any vocal ways that they are comfortable with, individuals who I had perceived as not being confident when chanting or singing as a class often created a new, interesting or unique response. The importance of giving individuals choices in response, rather than a closed response, is perhaps significant here. Having ownership of the vocal response and knowing that any form of vocal response was acceptable gave achievable criteria for success and thus a safety net for experimentation. Not everyone is more confident singing with others; some are happier on their own.

Two-note tunes

Songs made up of the sound of the playground call, the falling pitch sound of the cuckoo, the old-fashioned sound of a police car siren, the sound of the chime bars playing g to the e below (to be met again in Chapter 4) will be very familiar to you once you have heard it. Children will use this sound in their own singing, often mixed with speech, without anyone teaching it to them. As a natural song, small though it is, this can provide a very helpful bridging melody for game songs or children's improvised new songs.

Game songs are fun and a means of capturing children's participation and involvement for a real purpose. Songs which use children's names seem to appeal even more.

CLASSROOM STORY

Singing hats. Limited note game songs – vocal confidence and creativity

As part of a design and technology topic Tom's Year 4 class had designed and made a range of exotic and quixotic hats. The class were going to show their hats at an assembly but to introduce their creations to each other Tom intended to use a song. The class had not had much singing experience and he was building their individual singing confidence through game songs based on the falling minor third. The class already knew quite a few songs now and were familiar with the sound. Each child had brought their hat hidden in a carrier bag to a seated circle. This was the grand unfolding.

First Tom sang the whole song to the class with actions for the question, knocking rhythmically with closed fist onto open palm for 'Rat-a tat tat' and hand cupping ear for 'Who is that?' He then took out and put on his own, bought, felt jester's hat, complete with bells, out of a carrier bag for the answer. 'Mr Robson in his funny hat!'

Once the laughter had died down Tom encouraged the class to sing through the song with him.

Each child was then given time to get their hat ready to whip out of the bag and to think of an adjective to describe their hat. The game song then began. The class sang the question and the individuals in turn sang their own answers while showing their, funky, googly, spiky, flowery, cup of tea, mobile phone hats.

This naturally sung interval, the falling minor third, is the basis for much of the early singing work developed by the music educators Zoltán Kodály and Carl Orff. They both advocated that singing should be within an accessible, limited pitch range so that children are enabled to hear and control their vocal pitch accuracy at any age.

Actions and finger play

Physical movement accompanying singing can support freeing the voice and provide an intrinsic motivating factor. The actions can create a vehicle for children who are not confident with using their voices to still be actively involved. The movements themselves can make the singing easier, they can physically help. Actions can also provide a focus away from the voice, while confidence is building. Additionally, they can be useful visual and kinaesthetic reminders of what a song is about, what order the words or phrases come in and they can support memorising and learning lyrics. They might also create a pleasing body sounds accompaniment for the song.

There has been much recent educational debate concerning the importance of multisensory approaches to learning and the need to provide for children opportunities which stimulate both hemispheres of the brain. The activity of singing a song, words communicated through the voice employing the musical elements pitch and rhythm, of itself engages both hemispheres of the brain, the left hemisphere containing the vital skills of speech and the right processing musical pitch recognition. Adding movement not only enhances the learning experience but engages an additional learning process.

Movement learning is the oldest and most basic learning we experience and it can modify the effectiveness of both right and left brain learning. There is a great deal of research to show that movement learning is fundamentally important to humans, and that we begin to develop sophisticated thought processes in both right and left brain only through the medium of movement (Odam, 1995).

Finding the right level of challenge

Young children's attention is initially drawn to the rhythm and words of a song, not to the pitch which develops more gradually. In the early stages, building a joining in and having a go attitude is the priority. Physically, children's vocal range is quite limited in the Early Years and Key Stage 1, extending with physical maturation and vocal experience during Key Stage 2. While this does not mean that children will not enjoy and be able to participate in all sorts of songs, this feature needs to be borne in mind.

RESEARCH SUMMARY RESEARCH SUMMARY **RESEARCH SUMMARY** RESEARCH SUMMARY

The research concerning appropriate pitch ranges for children at different stages in their singing development is contradictory. Infant boys are most comfortable in the octave range between G and g across middle c. Infant girls prefer a slightly higher and wider range, just over an octave from A to b across middle c (Cleall, 1970). The best range for children between ages three and six is from middle c to the c an octave above (Forrai,1974). From personal experience I would question the breadth of this compass. Even with seven-, eight- and nine-year-olds I have found children's comfortable vocal range to be much more limited, with confident and able singers happily singing over an octave range. Vadja's (1986) contention that four- to five-year olds can usually sing a range of five to six notes, some only singing songs that encompass three to four notes, is a more accurate reflection of my experience. An average comfortable range is about d (above middle c) to g. Most children choose a range slightly lower than this. Opie (1985) observed that children seem inclined to choose a rather lower pitch than might be expected.

Why does it matter what an average comfortable range might be for children of any age? If singing development is to be viewed as an area of learning like any other, then the teacher will need some general awareness of what might present achievable challenges for the pupils. Children develop their singing through being appropriately challenged, but that they need to be presented with materials largely within their capabilities (Mills,1991).

Wider repertoire

A rich song repertoire is the recipe for children's motivation and interest, a wonderful way of connecting different areas of children's learning and experience and finding meaningful links across curriculum areas.

Specific suggested materials and resources for children at differing age phases will be addressed in Chapter 6.

A broad and balanced collection would include the following.

Nursery rhymes and traditional songs	*Hickory dickory dock*	
Repetitive songs	*Obwisana*	Ch 7
Call and response songs	*Day oh*	Ap'dix
Echo songs	*Tongo*	Ch 5
Action songs	*Slap the sillies out*	Ch 4
Cumulative songs	*One finger, one thumb keep moving*	Ap'dix
Counting songs	*Five little ducks*	Ch 7
Story songs	*There was a princess long ago*	Ap'dix
Songs in different languages	*Si tu aimes les maths*	Ch 7
Songs from different traditions	*Funge*	Ch 1
Pentatonic songs	*It's raining its pouring*	Ch 8
Rounds	*The ghost of John*	Ch 2
Partner songs	*A Pizza Hut and Pease pudding hot*	Ap'dix
Simple part songs (plus ostinato)	*Row, row, row your boat*	Ch 4
Pop songs	*Yellow submarine*	
Rap	In *Three Rapping Rats*	

Teaching songs

Initially concentrate on enjoyment, involvement, motivation and breaking down inhibitions. You can refine the sounds once you have the voices working.

Teaching by ear, face to face, without a piano gives invisible support.

- It encourages participation.
- It is easier to match another voice than another instrument.
- It avoids paper-shuffling.
- It encourages an energised, motivated response.
- It helps expression by providing a role model and vocal support.

As confidence grows, your voice should become gradually less, so that the singers can hear themselves and you can more clearly hear, and begin to assess, them.

To support this:

- find a repertoire which is appealing;
- ensure the pitch range isn't too wide and that the class will be able to manage it (don't forget that your voice is flexible, you can change the starting note and therefore the pitch to match the most comfortable one for your class);
- ensure the content, language and story of the song are appropriate to your class;
- add movement, actions or dance to free the voice;
- explore tongue-twisters for articulation, dropping the jaw for tone;
- try to make the song coherent and relevant to the lesson as a whole – use it to explore rhythms – use it to aid structure or stimulate composition – have the pupils write their own words, make up accompaniments – link this to music from a particular time, place, culture or style.

Decide on the best method of teaching the song

Generally begin by singing the tune as a whole for the children to listen to. This gives a holistic picture of the song. You can ask the children to listen out for particular features, e.g. places, names, story, events, mood, etc., to help focus and intensify the first listening.

If singing accurately is a matter of listening accurately then you might want to repeat this exposition asking the children to join in, in some way that is non-vocal. This will keep them involved and give them another chance to make sense of the structure of the song, e.g. tap the pulse, join in with an action or raise a hand when they hear a certain part.

The song can then be shared in a number of ways.

Echoing – you sing a line and the class repeat.

In a song of eight lines you might echo the first two lines then put them together. Echo the next two lines then put them together. This is called segmentation. Sing through the whole of the first half then the class copy and so on.

Absorbtion is the method by which we generally learn a song that attracts our attention on the radio or on audio CD. You hear the song, you join in with the bits you remember (usually the repeats or the bit you like best); you add to this gradually as you listen more intently to make out that phrase you can't quite catch. The class join in when they are ready or at the choruses.

Supporting the aural perception of the melody by showing the physical shape of the pitch using a hand sign can speed up the learning process and increase accuracy and it uses both the visual and kinaesthetic senses. This is good preparation for transferring the melody to tuned instruments or beginning to explore notation.

You can use a combination of these methods.

CASE STUDY

The Singing School Initiative – Maurice Walsh, Manchester Music Service

This project began in 2003 with a CD and songbook sent out to all Manchester schools in order to raise the quality and frequency of classroom singing. This has begun in Key Stage 2 with a series of fun songs which can be learnt and sung by children with minimum support from the teacher. One particular aim is to develop children's ownership and autonomy in singing. Children with particular enthusiasm for singing who have built their vocal confidence are encouraged to act as good singing role models and to lead the others as 'song bosses'. Schools are then brought together to have fun singing this common repertoire in a series of 'Singarounds'.

With the expansion of the project into Year 4 classes and in the light of the Wider Opportunities initiative which funds instrumental tuition, came the introduction of easy additional parts that can be played by instruments. Additional features are the inclusion of songs that support literacy, numeracy, 'brain breaks' and songs from the past.

CLASSROOM STORY
Sharing observations and experience

The golden rules for successful song teaching

Sarah, Lindsey, Gemma, Rachel, Jo and Kaye, all trainee teachers, had just completed their school-based training element of their third year. On return to university they discussed the approaches that they had taken in singing with their classes and the strategies that they had observed being used in school.

This is the guidance they produced as a support for their colleagues:

1. To choose songs children would feel comfortable with, i.e. not gender specific:
   – inclusion for boys, rap and connections with football chants;
   – inclusion of cultures by teaching songs from different cultures.
2. You need to be confident and to show enthusiasm. 'Enjoy it!'
3. You need to have a secure knowledge of the melody and lyrics of the song.
4. You must sing within the children's vocal range – not too high or low in pitch.
5. Sing the chorus first and build up the song. (Chorus should be repetitive.)
6. Get children to join in with any actions.
7. Remember to think about the structure of the song, e.g. teaching just one verse to begin with, rather than overwhelming the children with the entire song.
8. Encourage the children to join in when they are confident. If it is an action song only use actions at the beginning if they wish.
9. If necessary, slow down the song to begin with.
10. Don't move children on to the next step until each child is secure in their part.
11. Repetition is needed for consolidation.
12. Get children to try out a variety of parts.
13. When ready, introduce new parts and try variations.
14. Don't forget to appraise the children's singing, give positive feedback and discuss ways to improve.
15. Ensure you evaluate your own teaching to inform future planning – strategies that worked well or not so well and why.
16. Throughout the teaching week return to the song. Keep on top of the repertoire so that the children do not forget what they have learned. Keep a written record of learned repertoire yourself or create a class songbook.
17. At every stage give positive feedback.

A SUMMARY OF **KEY POINTS**

> **Recognition of singing as a skill that might be acquired rather than a gift bestowed at birth brings certain considerations.**

> **You need to build your own and children's singing confidence and competence, initially, through strategies for increasing motivation and involvement.**

> **It is important to be personally enthusiastic in your attitude toward singing.**

> **You need to identify repertoire which the children find accessible, appealing and fun.**

> **Some form of movement or action is useful to accompany the singing.**

> **Employ games as a means of singing for an enjoyable purpose.**

> **Make singing a positive, acceptable and usual form of communication in class.**

> **Find opportunities for children to contribute individually where they can, with the underlying failsafe that it is all right to say no if they do not wish to sing alone.**

> **Foster, implement and celebrate individual, as well as group development and success.**

The best possible environment for singing to be nurtured is one in which everybody sings – not just those with wonderful voices. (Hennessy, 1995, p31)

What next?

To build your own confidence and skills look for opportunities to join singing groups or choirs. Offer to join in with any singing clubs or groups in your placement schools. Many local authorities offer in-service training for music or singing courses for teachers. There are a number of organisations which offer regular training for teachers and children. Sing for Pleasure runs courses across the country and publishes an excellent range of resources. Look out for projects generated by the Music Manifesto (Sing Up) and Widening Opportunities initiatives.

REFERENCES REFERENCES **REFERENCES** REFERENCES **REFERENCES** REFERENCES

Cleall, C. (1970) *Voice production in choral technique*. London: Novello

Forrai, K. and Sinor, J. (1988) *Music in preschool*. Budapest: Corvin

Hennessy, S. (1995) *Music 7–11*. London and New York: Routledge

Mills, J. (1991) (revised edn 1995) *Music in the primary school*. Cambridge: Cambridge University Press

Odam, G. (1995) *The sounding symbol*. Cheltenham: Stanley Thornes

Opie, P. (1985) *The singing game*. Oxford: Oxford University Press

Umansky, K. (1998) *Three rapping rats – Making music with traditional stories*. London: A & C Black

Vadja, C. (1986) *The Kodály way to music*. London: Boosey and Hawkes

Useful websites

The British Kodály Academy: www.britishkodalyacademy.org.uk

The Orff Society UK www.orff.org.uk

Sing for Pleasure www.singforpleasure.org.uk

4
Key musical skills – Performing using instruments and other sound-makers in the classroom

By the end of this chapter you will begin to understand and know about:

- the potential of body sounds, untuned and tuned percussion and manufactured instruments as sound sources;
- a range of activities that make use of body sounds, untuned and tuned percussion;
- how to enable children to make simple instrumental accompaniments to songs or poems;
- how to lead activities that make use of instruments to explore the musical elements such as timbre.

This chapter addresses the following Professional Standards for QTS:
Q1, Q2, Q4, Q5, Q7(a), Q10, Q14, Q15, Q17, Q18, Q19, Q22, Q23, Q25(a,b,c,d), Q27, Q28, Q30

Body sounds

The simplest of all musical sounds are those made with our own bodies. These are used in dance and song routines in many folk traditions to provide rhythmic accompaniments.

When introducing these to children I would suggest leading with an example which models the qualities of what you expect the children to do. Only after that extend the ideas through the children's own explorations. Hence an activity for Key Stage 1 children such as a regular clapped pulse to accompany a well-known song could be developed by changing the sound to slapping thighs. Then children can be asked for their own ideas. Behind this particular progression is the teacher's provision of a supportive framework or 'scaffold', to use the Vygotskian (1935) term, within which the children are more likely to make purposeful progress while still being actively involved in creating, selecting and testing.

There is a range of exploring activities suitable for Year 1 children in Unit 1 of the QCA music scheme. One of these is intended to combine body sounds with vocal sounds, e.g. long sounds with the voice, short sounds with feet and fast sounds with hands. This is extended when children are encouraged to change the quality of the sound they make mid-performance, e.g. fast to gentle knocking or quiet walk to tip-toe and then on to stamping.

It is worth spending time with straightforward call-and-response activities to get a measure of the children's capabilities and to consolidate the 'vocabulary' of sounds and rhythm patterns they have created in the previous activity. This could take the form of creating patterns to a count of four, for example in the game 'Follow me' first mentioned in Chapter 1. The teacher performs a pattern such as the one that follows to a count of four.

tea coffee tea   tea

Then these can be varied to include a variety of body sounds or mixtures of sounds.

Coffee   coffee   tea   tea

Clap clap clap clap slap slap

The count of four is useful to maintain the momentum of the exercise.

Another way of practising body sounds is in the form of a song such as 'Slap the sillies out'.

Actions accompany the words 'clap' and 'wobble' and so on. Any actions can replace 'clap or slap' as the song progresses. Then these actions may eventually replace the singing of the action words 'clap or slap' altogether – thus developing a 'silent voice' as the children hear the action words in their inner ear.

PRACTICAL TASK PRACTICAL TASK PRACTICAL TASK PRACTICAL TASK PRACTICAL TASK

Learning objectives:

• To develop a vocabulary of sounds and rhythms.

• To become skilled at inventing and memorising rhythms.

Make four different patterns that each fit into a count of four. Each pattern should have at least two different body sounds within it. Memorise the sequence of four and repeat it a few times. Then create another sequence of four.

Try creating patterns which have one silent beat in the middle.

Below are some sounds that children can create with the body alone.

Full-handed clap	Toe tap	Cheek slap
Cupped hand clap	Foot stamp	Head tap
Hand rub	Two finger clap	Chest slap
Finger tapping	Fingers tapping	Tummy slap
Thigh slap		

A general reminder

You need to remember to keep the patterns of body sounds fairly simple and not too fast when working with Key Stage 1 children because they have yet to develop the gross motor control required for rapid movements.

Sound-makers

The word 'sound maker' has been used here to include both manufactured instruments and improvised instruments made from objects and materials ready to hand.

Untuned percussion instruments

These are instruments that have no specific pitch.

Drums

The most useful drums in the classroom are hand-held tambours, which are best played by tapping with the hard tips of two or three fingers on the opposite side to where they are being held. An instrument set should have at least three of different sizes (and having generally low, middle and high pitch). One very deep one like an Irish bodhran with a deep and strong tone is good to have to extend the timbral range. This draws attention to the tonal qualities of the instrument in contrast to its noisiness. Bongo drums have a bright tone and are easily handled by young children. Larger drums from North Africa such as djembe are good to have as a set if possible. North Indian tablas come as a pair. These are all played with the hands. The flat of the hand is generally termed a 'closed' sound, i.e. dampened, and the use of the tips of the fingers as 'open', a brighter sound. See Figure 4.1.

Drums with sticks such as a drum kit or samba drums are less useful for general purposes but may lead to more specialised (and more dedicated) music activity.

Slit or tongue drums are really closer in kind to wood blocks but are large and the beater (with a hard rubber end) should hit different 'tongues' on the top side to produce different pitches. Although the pitches are not precise, these instruments can produce something between a rhythm and a melody which is rather beautiful.

Tambourines are types of drums but with jingles attached. It is the jingles that are the distinctive sound of the instrument and when used with restraint can be very effective. In pop bands they might provide a continuous off-beat rhythm but generally a few beats are all that is needed. For best results a tambourine should be held still with one hand and struck with the moving hand on the opposite side of the instrument.

Rattles

Used in moderation these can be very effective. Pocket rattles are made with small pieces of wood secured to a leather strip and are played with a flick of the wrist. Other loud rattles I would keep well out of sight in general music lessons.

Bells, chimes and cymbals

Bells on a stick are the most controllable by children and therefore recommended. Agogo bells are specifically part of samba bands but have two bright tones that have a range of other uses. Sets of bar chimes make an entrancing sound and find their way into both popular and the most demanding art music. However, to be effective they need to be suspended on a stand. Small cymbals can be held in one hand and struck with a beater. The variety of sounds that larger cymbals can make if struck with different types of stick adds greatly to atmospheric effects but these are also better on a stand.

Figure 4.1 A tambourine and tambour being played with tips of the fingers. The djembe drum is played with a flat hand and cupped hand (see Chapter 6) and the most effective hold for jingles.

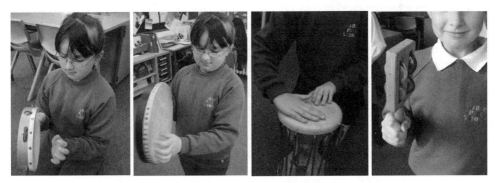

Scrapers and guiros

These make a gentle noise not unlike a frog and some are made in frog shapes; other louder ones are made to look like a fish. These can be scraped or struck and are therefore quite versatile. They are held by inserting fingers in two holes on the underside. Some come in the form of two wooden cylinders on a stick, which is easier to hold and can therefore have two tones as well – a very good investment.

Shakers, maracas

The most straightforward of these is a long closed cylinder with small beads inside, used in Latin American music usually with two hands by pushing backwards and forwards with double wrist action. A very loud instrument and hence not always to be recommended is a West African version made of a gourd with beads strung around the outside, called a shekere. Almost as loud and similar is the Latin American cabasa. Maracas are traditional but less easy to play in a controlled manner. In contrast are little hand shakers usually in the shape of an egg which, played like the cylinder, are more easily played rhythmically but are very easily popped in a pocket and forgotten about.

Figure 4.2 Untuned percussion playing techniques; guiro, shaker, capasa and ocean drum.

Tappers: wood blocks and castanets

Straightforward wooden blocks with a slit on the side when struck just above the slit make a beautiful, clear resonant sound and they are easily handled by children. Traditional castanets fall apart too easily but when fixed to a firm base (table castanets) are worth having in a classroom set. Two-tone wood blocks on a stick also make very good sounds and the *tick tock* is invaluable for sound effects or regular pulse sounds.

Blown instruments

The traditional blown instrument of the classroom is the recorder. It still holds its own as both an instrument worth playing in its own right but also as preparation for playing other more advanced instruments. More will be written about its contribution to extra-curricular music in Chapter 8. There are other blown instruments such as panpipes or melodicas that may have a place on the music trolley but have to be cleaned regularly.

Sound effects

A range of rather exotic sounding instruments have been invented or derived from world music originals. The vibraslap produces a sound like rattling teeth. The washboard became popular in skiffle groups in the 1950s and produces quite a good loud guiro-type sound. Ocean drums (see Figure 4.2 far right) and rain sticks speak for themselves with their names and the flexitone sounds rather like a musical saw.

Instruments for Early Years

Sets of small-sized instruments made from washable plastic with amusing animal shapes are clearly practical and attractive to younger children. Those who are concerned to buy robust instruments from sustainable sources will prefer small wooden instruments even if they are not as entertaining to look at.

Improvised instruments

Making sounds from everyday objects, at the same time as being economic, encourages creativity and resourcefulness. A large box of discarded containers and other potential sound-makers is a good start to a creative music lesson. Within this might be:

- tins (with any sharp edges filed down);
- wooden or hard plastic boxes;
- plastic pots. They make excellent little pitched drums. A set of varied sizes and shapes can sound quite as good as a very expensive tongue drum.

The same containers with rice or dried peas inside and a firm top make shakers as useful as commercial egg maracas but naturally not as durable.

Cardboard boxes or tins with corrugated surfaces to be scraped with a hard stick make guiro substitutes.

Creating an 'elastic band band' by stretching bands over firm boxes with different degrees of tension can be the basis of a good listening exercise.

The use of a sound table is particularly suitable to support this topic. Children may bring in to school sound-making objects and materials which others can be encouraged to experiment with to create sounds. These can then contribute to class projects. Figure 4.3 provides some sketches of untuned percussion instruments.

Figure 4.3 Identification sheet for untuned percussion instruments

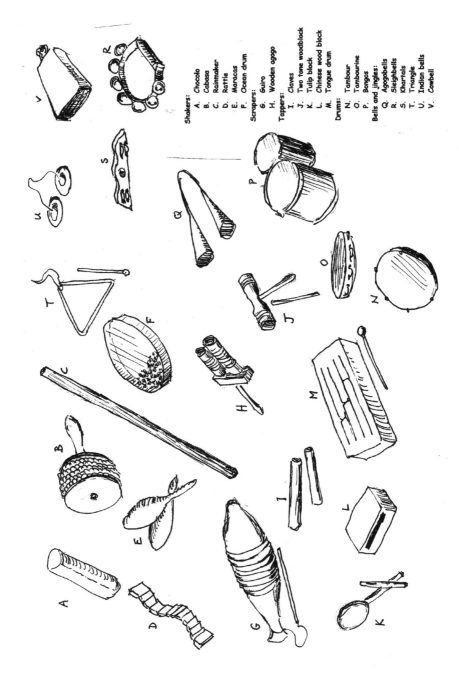

Shakers:
A. Chocolo
B. Cabasa
C. Rainmaker
D. Rattle
E. Maracas
F. Ocean drum

Scrapers:
G. Guiro
H. Wooden agogo

Tappers:
I. Claves
J. Two tone woodblock
K. Tulip block
L. Chinese wood block
M. Tongue drum

Drums:
N. Tambour
O. Tambourine
P. Bongos

Bells and jingles:
Q. Agogobells
R. Sleighbells
S. Khartals
T. Triangle
U. Indian bells
V. Cowbell

PRACTICAL TASK PRACTICAL TASK PRACTICAL TASK PRACTICAL TASK PRACTICAL TASK

Learning objectives:

• To realise the potential of everyday objects as sound-makers.
• To test out different ways of making sounds.

Put together your own collection of sound-makers from discarded containers. Look out for potential containers when doing the weekly shopping.

Classify them into: drums, shakers and scrapers.

Tuned percussion

Glockenspiels and metallophones and xylophones

Classroom glockenspiels are small and play in the soprano or alto range, with bars made of steel (*spiel* rhymes with *steel*). Metallophones are the deeper equivalent with a more rounded, bell-like tone. They have bars made of aluminium. There are also a full-range of xylophones which have wooden bars (*xylo* is Greek for 'wood').

These may be played with different types of beater to create different timbral qualities (see Figure 4.4). However, glockenspiels really need quite hard beaters to create a sound that carries well.

All instruments come in a standard range of notes, which is the scale of C major (equivalent to the white notes on a piano keyboard). For those who know about keys in music it is worth noting that they will have extra bars for F# and B♭ or may have the full range of sharps and flats attached.

Beaters

Beaters for tuned percussion range from soft to very hard.

Figure 4.4 A tuned percussion instrument being played with two beaters

Large beaters with a wool covering are very effective for metallophones and xylophones. There should also be a range of smaller beaters from soft rubber through to hard rubber or plastic to wooden for very bright hard-edged sounds.

It is best practice to require children to use a beater in each hand and hence to keep them in pairs if possible. The use of both hands in tandem is good both for co-ordination and to exercise both sides of the brain. Later it will enable much more nimble playing because the beaters will not have to leap about as much.

Maintenance

Often it is useful to remove the bars that are not required for a particular piece of music. It is a good idea to instruct children to remove the bars with a hand at both ends so that the pegs that hold them in place do not get damaged.

Electronic instruments

Electric keyboards extend the range of sounds achievable in a classroom if that is felt to be necessary. But the very important use is that they can produce non-percussive sustained sounds which none of the above can do except the blown instruments. This is a very important function. Also a keyboard can produce a wide range of ambient sounds which might provide background to a composition. Keyboards can also provide an automatic rhythm accompaniment to a class activity or a composition. See Figure 4.5.

Figure 4.5 A generic diagram of an electric music keyboard

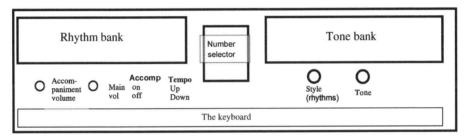

Making simple accompaniments

This should be read alongside Chapter 3 because, I suggest, accompaniments should become a regular part of developing songs in the classroom. The first accompaniments that you were introduced to in that chapter were vocal. At Key Stage 1 they need to be simple and to follow the song closely. The following is an example in which the instruments reflect the meaning and rhythm of the song.

Patterns can be similar to the rhythm of the song but not always imitating. In the following example the guiro rhythm *scrape tap* begins by accompanying the ends of the lines of the song but then becomes a continuous repeated pattern, or ostinato, at the end. In a similar way the percussion part in a rock group very often is repetitive but with additional features at the beginning or ending of a phrase.

The Animal Fair

Combinations of instruments make an ostinato more interesting.

The following traditional American rhyme lends itself to the addition of:

a rain stick

and a woodblock with a tambourine

Rhythm pattern:

It ain't gonna rain no more, no more

Percussion ostinato:

It ain't gonna rain no more,

z | ı ⊓ ı ⊓ | ı ı ı

How in the heck can I wash my neck

⊓ | ı ⊓ ı ı | ı

If it ain't gonna rain no more?

An alternative approach is to use percussion instruments that are deliberately varied and interspersed. Variety adds colour to the performance and makes a range of demands on the performers. Interspersing the sounds to illustrate the text requires the players to listen carefully for their cue words. Then they need to match the rhythm they play to the syllabic pattern of those words. In the next example, 'Tinga Layo', I hope less experienced readers will see where the accompanying instruments come in the song.

When teaching these accompaniments I suggest all the children are taught to clap the rhythm by rote and to play it on wood blocks. Then all the class sing the song and the wood block players join in when their words come in the song.

Wood block

Come lit - tle don - key come

The tambourine part, which is a long shake on *lay* and a tap on *yo*, can be taught in a similar way, perhaps using a drum roll on the knees to represent the shake.

Tinga layo – traditional Caribbean song

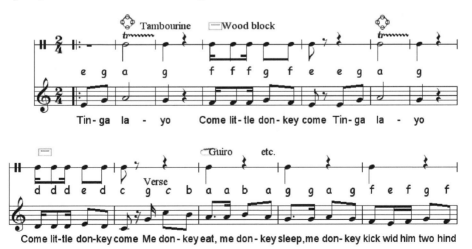

feet. Me don-key eat, me don-key sleep, me don-key kick wid him two hind feet.

Verse 2   *Me donkey walk*
        Me donkey talk,
        Me donkey eat wid a
        spoon and fork

Up to this point all examples have been about the use of untuned percussion. But the principles already established can be applied to the use of tuned percussion as well. A very simple song like 'It's raining it's pouring' can be accompanied by an ostinato of the two 'calling notes' G and E alternating throughout.

One player starts to play the regular G E ostinato. The songs fits to a count of 4 so after 4 or 8 beats the singers start.

Figure 4.6 chime bars or tuned percussion

PRACTICAL TASK PRACTICAL TASK PRACTICAL TASK PRACTICAL TASK PRACTICAL TASK

Learning objectives:

• To develop skill and confidence in use of instruments.
• To be able to create accompaniments using untuned percussion.

Select two words in the song, 'It's raining it's pouring' to accompany with two instruments. Consider particularly the timbre of the instruments. Consider one of these or an additional instrument to accompany the song all the way through. Will the sounds be rhythmic or more like a sound effect?

A more elaborate ostinato may be created from a simple chord. A major chord can be created by starting with the key note, let's say C, and building upwards by selecting alternate notes, thus:

Figure 4.7 Chime bars or tuned percussion

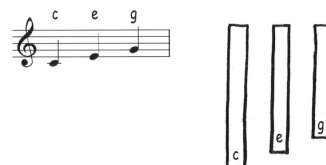

PRACTICAL TASK PRACTICAL TASK PRACTICAL TASK PRACTICAL TASK PRACTICAL TASK

Learning objectives:

• To develop skill and confidence in use of instruments.
• To be able to create accompaniments using tuned percussion.

Create an accompaniment to the well-known round 'Row, row, row your boat' by playing any four-note ostinato made from the notes of the chord of C.

The use of tuned percussion instruments for composing will be explored further in Chapter 5.

If the repeated pattern takes the form of two notes played together as a chord then this is called a drone. This is the accompaniment that supports the melody of a bagpipe for instance and such an accompaniment is traditional in Indian music also (played by the tanpura). In these cases the sound is continuous but when using tuned percussion such as a metallophone it would take the form of repeated chords. A drone does not suit all classroom songs. However, many rounds will sound well with this one chord type accompaniment because they are based on only one or two chords.

Instrumental performing and composing

Another form of accompaniment is to make background music to the recitation of a poem. The music is like a film backing track in the way it contributes to the character and mood of the poem.

PRACTICAL TASK PRACTICAL TASK PRACTICAL TASK PRACTICAL TASK PRACTICAL TASK

Learning objectives:

• To develop skill and confidence in the use of instruments.

• To realise the potential for exploring musical elements by creating background music using untuned percussion.

Using your own collection of sound-makers, create sounds to back a recitation of the poem below. Consider which of the musical elements you are exploiting in the different ways you play the sound makers.

Supermarket sounds

Squeak, squeak–squeak.
It's the supermarket trolley.
Blip, blip, blip.
It's the supermarket till.
Crash, crash, crash.
 It's the supermarket basket.
Ten pounds please!
It's the supermarket bill!

Christine Robson

Playing instruments may stand on its own as well as providing accompaniments to songs or poems. Making the whole class into a band can be a rewarding experience for the children as well as providing a model for smaller group activities. Such music is not reliant on the words of a song or a poem but has its own expression and structure. The whole class may be divided into groups, each with a distinctive kind of instrument or body sound so that the music will explore a variety of instrumental texture and timbres.

Children will become quite excited by both the prospect and the actual performance of instruments so the organisation, the distribution and the management during perform-ance is a very important feature of the lesson plan. These aspects will be considered in the section on planning and organisation in Chapter 8.

Teaching example

Learning objectives:

- To develop controlled performance on percussion instruments.
- To become more aware of the distinctive timbres of the instruments and the effect of varieties of texture.

The class, upper Key Stage 2, is divided into five groups:

- bells and triangles;
- woodblocks;
- shakers;
- drums;
- tambourines and jingles.

The teacher leads by presenting the chart below and pointing out which line each group should follow by pointing to squares at random and seeing if the appropriate group puts their hands up. Then she ensures that they can interpret the symbols. When all are ready she uses a long stick in a vertical position to drag slowly across the chart from left to right. As the stick meets the symbols applicable to each group they create the appropriate sounds. This may need to be rehearsed a few times until it works smoothly. A follow-up activity could be to create such a chart on an interactive whiteboard or overhead projector sheet with suggestions from the class. In effect this would be a 'shared composing' activity. The great benefit is that all the children have insight into the composing process.

Figure 4.8 A graphic score for whole-class or group performance

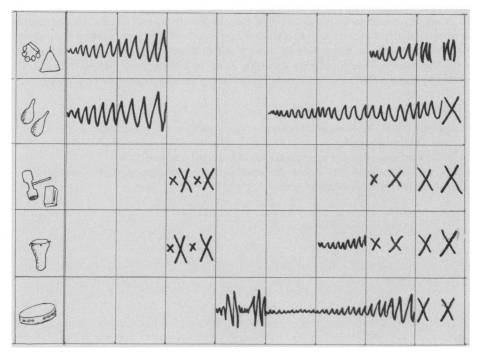

REFLECTIVE TASK
REFLECTIVE TASK

Learning objective: To understand the tension between organising enjoyable activities and behaviour management.

Very often student teachers will exploit the fact that children are excited by the thought of playing instruments as a control strategy. They may say, *If you are all well behaved then we may be able to play the instruments at the end of the lesson.* Consider where it might be a valid strategy to use but also what is lost by taking this line.

A SUMMARY OF KEY POINTS

> The musical resources at your disposal include body sounds and every day, often discarded, containers, as well as manufactured instruments.

> Children need time in a structured lesson to find out about the qualities of instruments.

> Similarly, they need to find out and to be instructed about effective ways of playing instruments.

> Making simple accompaniments are some of the best ways of using instruments to develop musical skills.

> Activities using instruments should include opportunities for the whole class and groups and will explore the musical elements of timbre and texture in particular.

What next?

Organising accompaniments to songs is quite demanding in itself. You will have done very well to have carried out one or two of these activities. However, the future of this type of activity depends on the capacity of the children to be sufficiently familiar with the use of such instruments that they can manage much of the organisation themselves. Also they may begin to see where different kinds of accompaniment would be appropriate for themselves. Such abilities can only arise in a classroom where they feel it is possible to make mistakes without criticism or being seen in a negative light by peers.

REFERENCES REFERENCES **REFERENCES** REFERENCES **REFERENCES** REFERENCES

DfEE and QCA (1999) *The National Curriculum – Handbook for teachers in England KS1 and 2* London: DfES Publications

QCA (2000) *A scheme of work for key stages 1 and 2 – music.* London: QCA

Vygotsky, L. (1935/1978) *Mind in society: The development of higher psychological processes.* Cambridge MA: Harvard University Press

5
Key musical skills – Creativity through composing

By the end of this chapter you will begin to understand and know about:

- **some definitions of creative characteristics and processes;**
- **the distinction between teaching creatively and teaching for children's creativity;**
- **some approaches for developing children's creative musical ability through composing.**

The chapter addresses the following Professional Standards for QTS:
Q1, Q8, Q10, Q14, Q24, Q25(a,b,c,d), Q27, Q28, Q30, Q31

Music and creative education

In recent years there has been a re-emphasis on the importance of ensuring that formal education is meeting society's future needs by encouraging and enhancing young people's creative development. The successful individual will require the ability to think and act in a creative manner.

Creative education involves striking a delicate balance between teaching knowledge and skills and encouraging innovation. More explicitly, creative education involves *forms of education that develop young people's capacities for original ideas and action*. (NACCCE, 1999, p4).

Seen in these terms, music has the potential to make a significant and valuable contribution. As an art form, music is often considered to be creative by definition. As a form of expression, music can provide an active and practical application for creative thought, a medium through which imagination can become a reality, a means by which ideas may be put into action. Creative abilities require a practical application for development to occur: listening and responding to music, performing music and in particular creating and composing music are all ways of giving form to thoughts, feelings and emotions.

Making music is often used as an exemplification of the process of creative thought production. The lively image of children playing a variety of parts on percussion instruments, singing with confidence and expression, immersed and absorbed in performing their part in a class composition may be clear evidence of motivated, successful, musical learning. However, the children's journey of development in musical skills, knowledge and understanding may or may not have been a creative one for them.

For the trainee teacher, handling creative exploration of music can pose a real challenge. Music, of necessity, must involve making sounds. Unexpected, incomplete, partially formed music in progress feels remarkably like noise. In the primary classroom noise levels have all sort of connotations. The trainee teacher may feel anxious when giving children space to pursue their ideas, or to experiment with sound, for fear of losing control and creating mayhem. Careful planning of organisation, establishing negotiated practices for distributing and handling instruments, establishing agreed parameters for sound levels and encouraging children to self-check that they are respecting the sound space of others and taking care of the sound instruments are important considerations (see Chapter 8). Attention to these details can create the structure and provide the control, security and reassurance that allows for risk taking and adventure within constraints for both teacher and pupil.

In light of these potential barriers, perhaps the first step in establishing a creative musical learning environment is having a positive attitude toward creativity. Recognising and believing that creativity is to be valued, both across the curriculum and in music, is vital. Without this, the potential for children's creative capacity cannot be realised. It is this attitude which is essential in working towards excellence (Glover and Ward, 1999, p15).

To value creativity we need first to attempt to define what we may mean.

In search of definitions

When faced with the question of what constitutes a creative person, many definitions spring to mind. For some, the creative individual is perceived as the genius, the exceptional artist or composer, the mad scientist or inventor; people whose historically original ideas and actions have led to the production of unique theories or artefacts.

Compared with these rare beings, the creative aspects of ourselves as individuals may appear to be as unattainable and distant as imagining that we are the architects of a fascinating new building or a vehicle which can conquer the boundaries of space. While we recognise that these feats of creative achievement are possible, by those with unusual gifts and talents, we may find it difficult to see ourselves within this elite definition.

For others, every individual is creative in some way. Creativity is perceived as a basic capacity of all human intelligence, the potential for creative achievement existing in everyone. In a democratic definition the creative attributes of being curious, asking questions, pursuing intentions, experimenting with ideas to solve problems, putting ideas into action are viewed as part of the human make-up. Young children are hard-wired for creative achievement. They are often way ahead of adults, as they instinctively think and act in spontaneous, imaginative and visionary ways, constantly asking 'why' and 'what if?' (Corri, 2004, p140).

We all have a predisposition to creative ways of thinking and behaving. To survive and thrive we regularly adapt and invent to meet, match or challenge ourselves and our circumstances. To solve real problems we look to our previous experiences, notice what others have done, draw on our skills and understanding, collaborate with others, take action to find solutions and new ways forward. We may often meet dead ends and take wrong turns, but necessity is a great motivator, driving the intention and generating the tenacity which feeds our ideas and may lead us to take unexpected or alternative routes.

The belief that to be human is to be creative is certainly a positive and inclusive one, but what do we mean by 'creative'? There appear to be particular qualities, attitudes and ways of acting associated with the term. How do trainee teachers define these?

REFLECTIVE TASK

Learning objective: To analyse what you feel may constitute creative attributes or behaviours.

Think about an individual who you know and who you regard as creative. Take a few minutes to think about what it is that makes them creative in your eyes. How do the following descriptions match your view?

University story
When asked to recall, visualise, then describe a creative child, a group of Year 4 trainees, thinking about children in their recent class context, came up with the following characteristics. The characteristics are in no particular order, nor are they intended to be judgemental. They are merely descriptions.

Creative children are:

inventive, spontaneous, expressive, confident, dominant, unusual, imaginative, strange, instinctive, unique, tenacious, individual, curious, inquisitive, distinctive, artistic, musical, risk-takers, impulsive, purposeful, adaptive, problem-solvers, experimenters, improvisers, testers, explorers, expressive, absorbed, stubborn, challenging, questioners, analytical, evaluative, responsive, open to change, flexible thinkers, not afraid to adapt or alter

Creative children have ideas which are:

new and unique to them, take a new slant on an existing idea, variations of an idea, unexpected, bizarre, alternative, unconventional, self-centred, inspiring for others

Creative children:

day-dream, visualise, make up things, argue, challenge the conventional view, reinterpret, make leaps of imagination, make connections, transform ideas, can be disruptive, speculate, reflect, analyse their ideas and improve them, try things out, make things, play around with stuff.

Characteristics of creative processes

Within a democratic view of creativity the National Advisory Committee on Creative and Cultural Education, NACCCE (1999), suggests that when individuals are being creative they are generally engaged in processes which involve using imagination, pursuing purposes, being original and judging value. To be fully realised each of these processes requires time for a series of phases to occur. Closely related to the stages of creative thought as defined by Wallas (1926, p80), these involve periods of preparation, incubation, illumination and verification.

The key characteristics recognisable in any creative process can be summarised by the mnemonic **PIVOT**.

Purposeful: imaginative activity is stimulated by having a meaningful purpose related in some way to our interests and passions. Our curiosity is caught and our feelings, emotions and intellect react as we analyse and harness our skills to service our intention and achieve whatever it is that we wish to produce or make. The strength of the intention, our ownership of the purpose, will have a direct bearing on our ability to sustain our endeavour and efforts as we pursue a journey of trial and error and deal with frustrations incurred along the way.

Imaginative: imaginative activity involves not just having ideas, but generating and pursuing them. Imaginative ideas may be unexpected, original, divergent or alternative. Imitation, derided from an elitist view as indicating a paucity of imagination, can actually be a very positive ally for stimulating the imagination. In 'playing' with something familiar we gain confidence in our ability to handle an idea, find out how an idea works, and this may lead to making new or unfamiliar connections or being more prepared to take risks. Unforeseen creative insights may occur as we expand the possibilities of a given situation by seeing it afresh, taking a new perspective, adding something innovative, reinterpreting or combining ideas or even applying the idea in a strange way or an unfamiliar context.

Valuable: the emotional intensity of satisfaction, joy and pleasure of achievement will be balanced and affected by the strength and personal investment of the original intention.

Ideas, actions, objects and solutions are in themselves neutral; it is the value invested in them by the creator or others, judged against their criteria for success that becomes significant. There may be a mismatch between what an individual may perceive to be of value and what is judged to be of value by others. Whatever criteria are applied, there is always an element of critical thinking and appraisal.

Original: this is perhaps the characteristic which comes most readily to mind at the mention of the term 'creative'. The distinction here is that an idea, the process of exploring the idea or the product achieved may not be historically original or unique, but may be original to an individual when compared to their previous work. Similarly, when compared to others from a similar group the originality of an individual may become more apparent.

Time: this is vital for our conscious and subconscious selves to make deliberate or intuitive connections. We need space to consider intentions, to allow ideas to formulate. To pursue purposes, we need time to reflect upon the skills and knowledge that we have and compare this with what we may need. The opportunity to play with ideas in a concrete form, to draft and redraft, to reflect upon and evaluate each stage is paramount.

Additionally the NACCCE (1999) emphasise that:

- creativity can be expressed collaboratively as well as individually;
- creative possibilities are pervasive in the concerns of everyday life, its purposes and problems;
- creative activity is also pervasive: many people who are being creative do not recognise that this is what they are doing.

Creative teaching requires creative teachers. As a trainee teacher your creative self-image is important. Do you see yourself as a creative person?

REFLECTIVE TASK

Learning objective: To recognise personal creative activity in everyday situations.

Try to recall and visualise your individual response to the questions below.

If you can't think of an actual event for one question after a few minutes of pondering, go on to the next and come back to the unresolved question after a break, doing something else or after sleeping on it.

When is the last time you asked yourself *what would happen if…?*
When is the last time you approached a usual task in an unusual way?
When is the last time you had an opinion or an idea that seemed totally off the wall to everyone else?
When is the last time you took a risk?
When is the last time something or someone inspired your curiosity?
When is the last time you made something that you hadn't before?
When is the last time you helped a friend by seeing their situation or problem from a new perspective?

Don't worry if you couldn't think of events for every question. The main point is that you have been actively considering what it might look like to be thinking or acting creatively.

Try the exercise again, but this time relate the questions specifically to your university or school-based training. Hopefully, there will be a number of occasions to analyse if teaching and learning are, for you, creative processes.

Teaching creatively and teaching for creativity

Implied in the democratic view of creativity, that *all people are capable of creative achievement in some area of activity provided conditions are right and they have acquired the relevant knowledge and skills* (NACCCE, 1999, p28), is the notion that creativity can be taught.

Teachers can be creative in their own teaching; additionally and distinctly they can also promote the creative abilities of their pupils. The two are often connected but not necessarily synonymous. In teaching for creativity the teacher's roles are to recognise young people's creative capacities; and to provide the conditions in which they can be realised.

The creative teacher

While recognising that there will be as many interpretations of the term 'creative teacher' as there are teachers, the following statements provide a useful basis for reflection and debate.

Creative teachers:

- engage in creative thinking and creative processes themselves;
- recognise, nurture, nourish and employ their own creative muscles to enable them to teach in creative ways;
- see themselves as active learners and problem-solvers;
- are curious about teaching and learning in all sort of contexts and ways;
- ask themselves *what would happen if…* and then try it out;
- research and continually update their own knowledge, skills and understanding;
- ask questions and pose problems about ways of learning and teaching;
- have masses of ideas and actively seek out the ideas of others;
- adapt and transform ideas to meet their own purposes;
- analyse children's needs, recognising the diversity of children's knowledge, individual skills, the levels of their conceptual understanding and importance of connecting with their interests and passions;
- have the will, courage and commitment to try out many approaches;
- experiment with teaching styles, strategies, resources and organisation to meet children's needs;
- analyse the impact of their teaching on children's learning;
- see mistakes as an important part of learning;

- eagerly and consistently seek out imaginative, original and unusual ways to inspire children, to capture their interest, to generate excitement in learning and motivate their desire to learn;
- use personal anecdotes and real-life situations to animate a real desire for learning and to make learning meaningful;
- make all sort of connections between their life experiences, out of school experiences and their teaching; between areas of the curriculum;
- see potential in collaborations, situations and in people;
- employ multi-sensory approaches which engage learners in a variety of ways of being and knowing: the oral, aural and kinaesthetic alongside the visual;
- create, find and use inspiring, imaginative resources;
- structure learning opportunities in sequences and scaffold experiences which are designed to help children to achieve success;
- have faith and confidence in their pupils and high but realistic expectations which they make explicit;
- create a supportive environment where having a go is important and children's attempts are of value;
- are interested in and concerned to know what children think and feel, they seek out children's views and build in spaces for their voices to be heard and acted upon. They use this insight as inspiration for their teaching.

REFLECTIVE TASK
REFLECTIVE TASK

Learning objective: To analyse features of teacher creativity within a musical context.

Consider the following classroom story.
What evidence of creativity do you recognise in Laura's story?
How is Laura being creative as a teacher?

CLASSROOM STORY
Teacher creativity in action

Laura had planned to begin her Year 3 unit of work on using descriptive sounds by providing a range of activities, using untuned percussion instruments, which focused on the children experimenting with sounds and appraising the different ways the sounds could be made. Laura wanted to ensure that the children were aware of five ways of playing: by striking, shaking, blowing, plucking and rubbing. She had decided to set the children a challenge. As a group could they beat the 'seven sounds' challenge with their collection of sound-makers? Laura had seen the class teacher using a similar idea when encouraging the children to concentrate carefully and investigate thoroughly to find more than seven shades of colour in art, by experimenting with colour blending. The 'Seven shades challenge' had become the 'Seven sounds challenge'.

Laura had pondered on the idea of setting the context as a game show, but wasn't very familiar with organising working with the instruments and had not really handled children working with sound as media before. So she decided not to overcomplicate things.

When she went to collect the instrument trolley at the end of the morning, in preparation for her afternoon lesson, she found that the instruments were being used all week by another class.

Laura had already told the children they were going to be experimenters with sound; she had set an expectation that they would have great ideas and be able to make sounds in lots of different ways. She now had a problem: eager, curious, motivated children anticipating an experience but no instruments.

She remembered that in university sessions she had been encouraged to think of everything as a potential sound-maker; the objects in a room, the room itself, the surfaces, the furniture… She had already used body percussion with the children, so that wasn't new for them – one category of sound media dismissed! She needed inspiration. Sitting in the classroom Laura looked at the work the children had been doing on recycling. She had already sung a recycle song with them and they had made a 'Rethink, reduce, reuse, recycle' rap. The class had collected a whole sea of different papers. Newspapers of different sizes, glossy magazines, catalogues, junk mail, used wrapping paper. It was already sorted on the shelves into neat piles ready for remaking into papier maché, colour collages, mixed media compositions or contributing to the school paper recycling bin.

Could this be the sound media? Laura was worried that the children wouldn't be very impressed by these potential sound sources; she needed something to hook the children in and to make the materials have meaning, relevance and value.

She very quickly typed a letter and put it in an envelope to read to the children as the initial stimulus for her lesson. It read:

> Calling all creative kids in Key Stage 2. The council needs your help. We need you to compose a piece of music from waste papers to accompany a 30-second educational DVD on the importance of recycling all of your paper waste. We need your music. The title is 'Layers of paper', the sounds are up to you. Send your recordings to…

Eureka!

Postscript. Each group audio-recorded all of the sounds that they had found and made with a variety of papers, just as evidence that they really had made more than seven. In addition, each group recorded their layers of paper composition. Having listened to the recordings to appraise not only how the sounds were made, but the sounds the children liked, the ones they found surprising or interesting, the sounds they were intrigued by, the children asked if they could make a class recording of the 'seven sounds challenge'. This inspired Laura to go and find out from the ICT co-ordinator if there was a way the children could loop the sounds to make a class 'layers of paper' composition. There was. The ICT co-ordinator also introduced Laura to a useful program. You will find a version of this idea later in this chapter in 'Creative ways of using a keyboard'.

A creative teacher will implicitly be teaching for children's creativity through modelling creativity. In many respects the attributes and values of a creative teacher will also underpin teaching for creativity – perhaps just a change in intention or perception is all it takes.

Teaching for creativity

In teaching for creativity the emphasis is a shift toward fostering conditions, creating opportunities and making explicit to children what being involved in a creative experience looks like and feels like.

Teaching for children's creativity involves:

- perceiving children as creative, unique individuals who are naturally curious and designed for experimenting, who will seek amazing and surprising paths toward achieving a goal if given the right hook;
- providing stimuli which stoke children's curiosity, grab their attention, and get their imaginations buzzing;
- giving children the message, loud and clear, that you believe in their potential to be a creator, an artist, a composer;

- equipping children with the tools to achieve this and celebrating when they are taking part in the process even in the smallest way;
- encouraging children to have the confidence to try;
- noticing where children's particular interests, talents and aptitudes seem to lie and nurturing and finding other avenues for them to expand upon these;
- valuing open-endedness;
- giving children the option to make choices, try alternatives and helping them to understand what may be appropriate choices within particular circumstances;
- being prepared to create small, secure spaces for children to make real decisions and have real ideas that are taken on board, valued and acted upon, not just paid lip service to;
- helping children to make connections and envisage what might be;
- letting children go with their idea, even if you can see it won't work; encouraging them to try it out, not to worry if it doesn't work first time;
- relinquishing a level of control to the children, preparing them for this and entrusting them with it;
- setting up situations where the outcome is genuinely unknown, may be surprising, may succeed or perhaps more importantly may fail – children need to see a variety of ways of handling setbacks and using this to move on;
- being ready to recognise frustration and dead ends and help children to cope with these as part of learning;
- coaxing children to hang on in to give problems chance to incubate; encourage them to leave it until another day, come back to it and help them to know about their subconscious brain working on it while they do something else;
- understanding that creative learning takes time and that the initial excitement of the stimulus, the experimental quest, will need to be balanced by time to reflect and think;
- discussing success criteria with children and encouraging them to explore and explain what they value, how they decide what they mean by 'good'.

REFLECTIVE TASK
REFLECTIVE TASK

Learning objective: To make connections between 'teaching for creativity' in general and 'teaching for creativity' in musical terms.

Playing with sound through improvising is one way in which we might involve children in the process of composing. How many aspects of teaching for children's creativity can you recognise within Christine's story below?

CLASSROOM STORY
Taking risks together

Christine was looking forward to her first Year 6 music lesson. The class teacher had explained that the children had regular opportunities to use the instruments with the teaching assistant who usually took them for music. They liked music and dance and enjoyed music with a 'bit of a beat or a funky rhythm'. In art, the children were encouraged to share ideas, plan to research and follow through their own interests related to a particular artist, media or process as the teacher was very confident and passionate about this area of the curriculum, but they had very structured, teacher-directed lessons in music.

As a music specialist, Christine felt confident that she could engage the children in some open-ended music-making. She wanted to see how the children responded; she also wanted to gain some awareness of where the children were in terms of musical skill: how would they control their playing, could they handle improvising, could they listen and respond to each other, what would individuals show? Christine was also concerned with trying to teach for children's creativity, this was an area she had become quite passionate about and intended to focus on for her final year research study.

Prior to the lesson Christine had arranged the chairs in a circle and had placed a percussion instrument under each chair, to save time and have a prepared organisation for distributing the instruments. There were spare instruments in the centre of the circle and a beater bucket, in case any of the children were really uncomfortable with their given instrument and wanted to change it.

The lesson begins. Christine tells the children about the good things she has heard about them; she knows they like moving to rhythms and asks if they might enjoy playing some too. The children are very keen to do this. They tell her that they played some rhythms to words in Year 5 but haven't this year. Christine commends the children on their positive approach and their willingness to have a go. She also states that she wants the children to all take part in and enjoy the music sessions, but she does not want them to feel uncomfortable. All each child needs to do is their best; if something seems too difficult or uncomfortable then they should have a try and just do what they can, that's fine.

Christine then directs the children to look under their chairs and find the sound-maker placed there. The instruction is *see what you can get it to do*. After 20 seconds she stops the group, praising the children for being so alert and responsive to her red, circle-stopping signal. Christine asks the children to show a thumbs up if they have found a sound that they like and that they would be able to play even a tricky rhythm on, like the rhythm of the syllables of the words, 'Year 6 are incredibly brilliant!' Everyone has found a sound of some description and all make a successful attempt at playing their 'brilliant' rhythm phrase. Christine then explains that together they are going to make some music that has never, ever been performed before because it doesn't yet exist; it will be a piece unique to them. She tells the group she is excited by this, curious about what will happen and a bit anxious because she has never done this before and doesn't know what will happen. She also acknowledges that some of the children might feel a bit like this when they are thinking about or feeling what to play. Christine encourages the children to just have a go in some way. She tells them not to worry what their idea sounds like at first, just to feel their way into the music. They can play in any way they want as long as they respect the instrument and each other.

Christine begins to play a rhythm pattern which matches with the rhythm of the spoken words 'Double D, Three T, S and P' (the initial letters of the musical elements) on a metal agogo, she asks the children to listen, then to join in, in any way that they want on their instrument.

After about 20 seconds most of the children are playing. The child sitting directly opposite Christine is conspicuous by her stillness: she is not playing anything at all, she isn't looking anxious, but she isn't relaxed either. The other children play tentatively at first then get a little louder, some play the same pattern as Christine, some play a pulse, some play all the time, some just play now and again, some stay with the first thing they tried, some change their pattern a few times, some appear to be playing to fit in with the person sitting next to them. Just toward the end of the piece, which lasts for about four minutes, the still child begins to play very quiet, random sounds on her indian bells. The piece feels as though it is coming to an end when children start to look around at each other. Just as the tension begins to be too much one child gives a big crash on her cymbal and everyone instinctively stops. A whole variety of different, individual choices and responses are in play, and a new percussion ensemble piece is born.

After the experience Christine asks the children to describe what they did, the decisions they made, what they liked or didn't about the newly made piece and why. She makes a particular point of asking Carole, the 'still' child who didn't appear to be well engaged. Carole says *I liked the sound of my indian bells, but they were going to get lost if I played at the same time as your metal sounds. So, I decided to wait until I could hear a little space where my sound could be heard on its own. I had to listen really carefully. There was only one little space and it was very small, it didn't happen very often so I had to keep listening out for it and listening for patterns to see where it came. I'd just begun to be able to play in my space when we finished.* Christine is totally taken aback. She had judged Carole's response as lacking playing skill and confidence, not showing musical skills or understanding. It was apparent from her answer that the opposite was true.

Composing

Composing in music means selecting and using musical skills to explore musical ideas, forms or structures in light of a stimulus or with an intention. It involves enacting ideas and trying out possibilities. It might involve drafting and redrafting in light of the desired outcomes and making judgements about what is successful and why. The product of the process is fixed in some way, through repeating, through memorising or through recording in visual form. These elements are clearly recognisable in creative terms.

Composing opportunities need to be planned as part of children's ongoing skills development in music. The teacher also needs to be alert to opportunities for composing which may arise in the course of children's everyday experience in and out of school. This requires open, acute observation of what children notice, enjoy, talk about and respond to. The teacher will need to see potential composing stimuli in other areas of the curriculum and make connections that will help children to do the same. Equally important is the need to give children opportunities to select and follow through their own composing intentions. This is often achieved as individual or group decisions within the broader, teacher-set parameter of a task, i.e. freedom for choices and decisions within a structure, or these could be entirely child generated.

A sound-rich environment

To have ideas and be able to make decisions in music children need to have a wide variety of experience of sounds to recall, recapture and imitate. To enable children to develop a sense of sound as potential media at their disposal, and music as a way of making things up, the learning environment needs to contain sound media, and be sound rich. Of course voices and bodies are always available, but, as Laura's story showed, everything around could be conceived of as potential sound media. To draw a parallel with the visual arts, drawings, paintings and sculptures can be made through observation, exploration and response to anything. Teachers will often include ideas for making in visual media as an instinctive part of any themed learning experience. Composing music and using sound media are not so instinctively part of the teachers' repertoire. Perhaps the first step towards you facilitating children in this experience is to begin to be more alert to using sound as an expressive medium and composing as a way of putting sound ideas into practice.

Improvising

Much of the composing activity which takes place in primary classrooms could be described as supported improvisation. Finding ways of playing different sounds on any instrument by trying out what the instrument can do is a mini improvisation in action. Practising controlling sounds as part of performing is a dynamic and very common way into composing. If composing is about experimenting with sounds within different structures, for particular purposes, a form of musical play, then the trial and error of the improvising process can be a potential way in. The teacher may model a particular idea inviting the children to copy or adapt the idea themselves. More often than not, the children may be thinking and playing on the spot. They will be showing their instinctive response and reacting in real time. This can be an exciting and stimulating experience or can feel a little scary.

Teaching for creativity recognises that perhaps the greatest inhibitor to any creative endeavour is fear of failure. Children's tentative explorations require small, frequent opportunities within a safe, structured, supportive environment where the challenge is high but threat is low.

For this reason short, frequent, supported, invited experiences, within a supportive climate are necessary to build both confidence and competence. In all instances providing children with a 'get out' clause, giving them valid permission to 'pass' can give them control when deciding whether they are ready to have a go or not.

Composing in the primary classroom is often a class or group activity, but individual opportunities are also important. In the Early Years setting, this will involve setting up indoor and outdoor access to sounds to play with, just like sand, water or apparatus.

A frequently changing sound table can give scope for individual experimenting at any age.

Generating ideas

Ideas rarely occur in a vacuum. Children need practice in having ideas, and teachers need practice finding ways to encourage children to have them. Giving value to children's ideas in themselves, in a non-judgemental way, can help to toward building a climate where children are eager and expected to have a view and can feel confident in expressing an alternative way. Many and varied opportunities to imitate a wide range of ideas, modelled by teachers, peers and others are fundamental for children to be able to formulate their own ideas.

Glover (1998, p143) makes the case that much of children's learning begins with observation of the activity of those around them followed by efforts to recreate what they see. As a wellspring of creative activity, imitation is fundamental in nurturing the imagination. It is in the process of imitation that ideas are remade, interpreted and perhaps transformed. The process of reconstruction is a creative act in itself, allowing movement from the known to the unknown. Imitation is a major catalyst in children's compositional development.

Stimuli
Potential stimuli for children's composing might include some of the following:

- games;
- pictures;
- objects;
- stories;

- poems;
- events;
- soundscapes of particular places or environments, real, visited, remembered or imagined;
- pieces of music;
- musical structures;
- moods;
- feelings;
- the properties of particular instruments, e.g. keyboards.

Whatever the stimulus, the musical materials at the children's disposal will be strongly linked to the musical **elements**, the range of sound media or **resources**, the **intention** and purpose of the composer and the **context** in which the composition is to be made or played. When guiding initial discussions with the children, constructing questions to generate ideas or to drawing attention to potential ways forward these features are worth remembering. The mnemonic **ERIC** is a useful tool both for you and the children.

Games

Musical games provide an excellent vehicle for creative decision-making, child-differentiated skills practice and opportunities for both improvisation and composition within a structure, but with room for invention. Variations are expected, providing an accessible and purposeful way into 'making something individual and new' from a given original, for a real and valid purpose. Peers will often readily assess a game for the creator in light of their own criteria: *this is fun, easy, hard, brilliant, boring!* The negative analysis has more chance of generating a redeeming idea from the other players such as: *Why don't we? I think it would be better if. What would happen if?* Critical analysis and judgements can be more acceptable and give children the experience of handling a bad press or negative comments within a virtual situation, much like role play.

The teacher can model the initial idea. The children learn how the game works. Through observing the children's participation, the teacher gains some idea of the children's levels of confidence or competence in the particular musical skills or ideas, and can also provide support for the personal and social elements of the rules for playing. In light of the intention to give children every opportunity to contribute, it is important to invite their contributions from the outset, raise the expectation that they are bound to have other, better ideas, even before you have played. This preparation will provide the chance for children to be playing the game with a view to imagining and expressing their own ideas; a good precursor to their own invention.

PRACTICAL TASK PRACTICAL TASK PRACTICAL TASK PRACTICAL TASK PRACTICAL TASK

Learning objective: To learn a musical game and to consider new ways of adapting this.

Set yourself a steady pulse. Chant the words of the game song below until they feel rhythmical and natural. Look at the pitch positions of the words. Can you imagine the tune? Sing your own version of the tune.

Get a small glockenspiel, then find the notes and play the tune as it is written.

Now, you choose which tune you are going to use. Sing it a few times so that you feel confident.

A three-note game song

---

			a	

Lis-ten to | Lis-ten to | Can you | my pa- |
this! | This? | play | ttern? |

Make up some actions to accompany the song. At the end of the song clap a steady rhythm pattern, to a count of 4. You now have the material for an echo game.

You are the composer. How could you vary this game as it stands?

The pattern in this version is all about rhythm in four and uses a particular body percussion as the sound-maker.

What other patterns could the game explore?

Think about the musical elements, sound resources, different intentions and contexts to explore your own variations.

Here are a few ideas to start you off.

1. Change the words of the song to *Listen to this, listen to this, can we play your pattern!* Give the lead to any child who would like it. They use your model, but they now have to think of the patterns. (*Tip* – when playing rhythm patterns in 4 make the first pattern a straight 4, i.e. ▌ ▌ ▌ ▌ . This gives everyone a feel of how long the composing space lasts and sets an aural, visual and kinaesthetic model of that space.)

2. Pass a tambour around as the song is sung, while you keep a gentle pulse of four on a second tambour. When the song stops, whoever is holding the tambour copies the pattern individually. (*Tip* – always give solo players the chance to pass on their turn if they wish to.)

3. Give children chance to play the game themselves in pairs or to work in a group playing the game, each taking the role of leader.

Ask for new ideas for the game. Set this as a homework task.

Think about using tuned percussion to make patterns: on single notes, pairs of notes, particular combinations of notes, falling minor thirds, pentatonic scales, single notes on recorders, using chime bars or sung patterns.

The list is endless.

Try out your game in school.

Ask children to predict what you are going to do at the end of the song and what they will be doing. Listen to their ideas and acknowledge them. If one matches what you were going to do, celebrate this and use it. Remember and note down the children's ideas for later; these could be the first ways into individual interpretations. Notice who already has ideas. How easy will they be? Are they better than your intended game in terms of more challenging skills, more interesting approaches, better organisation or a variation you would never have thought of? Find ways to let children try these out. Help them to test their ideas and get some feedback from others. Make a musical games ideas book which could be in written text with symbols or a camcorded DVD.

When playing the game begin by taking the lead yourself. Notice how accurate the children are in echoing. If there are inaccuracies, repeat the pattern to give children further chances for practice and success.

Stories

The storyteller is a welcome member of any group. Children are familiar with and create stories from an early age, the level of sophistication developing with their life experience and skill with expressive language conventions. Most aspects of film and TV are simply stories being told in a technically visual medium. The tradition of story is as an oral medium. Many stories will include a number of features that are designed to keep the listener attentive and these can be very helpful for the budding composer. In addition, the telling of stories is often accompanied by the use of a hand-held instrument, a drum, a rattle or a fiddle.

When using story as a stimulus the following features may be worth focusing on.

Setting

Look for stories that have distinct settings which are described in very rich detail. For younger children very noticeable sounds in the setting will trigger ideas, especially if the setting is within their own experience, e.g. the playground, the street, the nursery, inside, outside or the farm. Older children will be able to transform visual images as well as sound images. The children can create the soundscapes to set the scene for the story to be told in different settings, to another class, to the whole school or to parents. As with other areas of learning, moving from the concrete to the abstract, or the real to the imagined, is a useful progression.

Characters

Describing the way a character looks is not, necessarily, the first feature easily expressed through music. Movements and emotions, or personality, are much more accessible. Contrasts and opposites can help children to see characteristics that they might play more easily. The huge, lumbering elephant will sound very different from the tiny, scurrying mouse; the ethereal, airborne elf, light enough to sit on a cobweb, will sound distinctly different to the gollumpy, land-bound, heavy dwarf, and grandad's slow shuffle sounds different from mum's businesslike stride. Even the youngest children will be able to show you, through movement and sound, very strong and obvious emotions as long as they can recognise those emotions in themselves. Lots of opportunities for using the instruments in circle time for 'play me how you feel today' activities can benefit children, not only in learning to express emotion but as another small step in the improvising and composing developmental experience.

Events

Creating a rumpus or a straw house falling down will be within the imagination and skill of most children. Journeys and travelling can provide multiple areas to think about. Forms of transport maybe involved, the roaring, spluttering engine of the old banger, expressed easily with the *vroom* of the voice, the urgent siren of the ambulance, screeching to a halt or the humming of the electric train all conjure up very obvious sound images. Travelling which involves climbing up and down is an ideal opportunity for children to improvise with pitch.

Teaching example

The teacher has an alto xylophone turned on its end with the long, low keys at the bottom and the short, high keys at the top. She has three beaters ready, one medium sized with the head carefully wound with green wool, one smaller than the others with a boy's-face head, one bigger than the others with a giant's-face head. The children are seated around the teacher on the carpet, listening intently as she tells their favourite story of Jack and the Beanstalk. When she gets to the part where the beanstalk begins to grow, the teacher uses her green-headed beater and, starting at the bottom of the keys, begins to play each note in turn. As the beanstalk grows higher and higher, the notes played get higher and higher. When the beanstalk disappears out of sight, the playing has got to the very top of the xylophone and then stops. When Jack climbs up the beanstalk, the same thing happens, but this time it is the small beater with Jack's character that does the playing.

Just before the exciting finale arrives and Jack is followed down the beanstalk by the giant, the teacher pauses in the story and asks the children if they can suggest how she might play her xylophone. She helps the children to notice that climbing up the beanstalk Jack started at the bottom like she did. She asks the children if the notes are high or low at the bottom. All the children know they are low. The children explain that to make 'coming-down sounds' the teacher will need to start at the top and play the steps all the way to the bottom. The teacher takes the green-headed beater and plays as the children instruct. *Is this how you want it?* asks the teacher. One child points out that she should really be using Jack's beater to come down. Another suggests that she'll have to come down very fast or the giant will catch Jack. A third says, *I think Jack will jump the last bit*. The teacher asks this child if he could come and show her how he wants the sound on the instrument to be. He begins at the top, plays down in step quite quickly, but with three keys still to go jumps the beater to the wooden frame at the bottom of the instrument. *What a wonderful way of playing your idea. I can practically see Jack scrambling down, quickly but carefully, like you played. Then getting impatient at the end and jumping off before the bottom. Just like you. Well done*. Tantalisingly, for the children, the teacher doesn't finish the story; instead she tells the children she is going to set the xylophone beanstalk and the three beaters up on the music table. She wants the children to go to the table in pairs over the next few days and to make up the final part of the story themselves.

Dialogue

To engage the audience, give the storyteller a break and the listeners a chance to join in, many stories have repeated phrases or rhymes usually with a strongly rhythmic character. These can be very accessible stimuli to make into vocal chants, in unison, in alternate parts or in layered parts. The durational values, the long and short sounds and silences created by the rhythms of the words can be directly copied onto untuned or tuned percussion instruments to great effect.

Poems

Rhythm and metre are common to many forms of music and poetry, though not all. The pulse of a poem as spoken and felt can be moved to, or actions composed for. Many teachers play the pulse of a poem on an instrument to help children to distinguish this aspect from the long and short rhythm patterns of the word syllables. Each of these elements of duration can be expressed musically. The content and mood of the poem can be the focus for composition (see 'Supermarket Trolley' in Chapter 4 and 'Burney's Hill' in Chapter 8).

Made-up rhymes related to a current topic and structured into a chant with a question and answer can be a supportive vehicle for encouraging individual spoken improvisations which can be transformed into played rhythms on any sound-maker.

Teaching example

The class are using selected pieces of music from Saint-Saëns's *Carnival of the Animals*, as a stimulus for creative work in poetry, art, music and dance.

The children know the animals that Saint-Saëns portrayed, including some rather unexpected animals like 'pianists' and 'fossils'. The class is sitting in a circle, which the teacher is part of. A collection of 30 percussion instruments is arranged as an inner circle and a bucket of beaters is in the centre of the circle.

The teacher chants the rhyme to a steady pulse which he taps on his leg.

Saint-Saëns made a carnival,
A carnival of animals.
Let's join the carnival.
What is your animal?

The children join in as much as they can the second time. By the third time they've all got it. They have also copied the teacher's pulse playing. The teacher explains that everyone is going to say the whole chant first to feel good and to warm up. After that the class chants the question then leaves a space lasting a count of four pulses for each person to choose and say their own animal. The teacher models the structure. Everyone chants the whole rhyme, chants the question and then in the space the teacher answers. He does a few examples to give ideas and to help the children to have enough repetition of the composing space (the four pulses) for them to feel comfortable with it.

All   *What is your animal?*
Solo   *A hairy orang-utan!* [He also adds actions and an 'oo oo' vocal sound.]
All   *What is you animal?*
Solo   *A teeny squeaky mouse!*

He then asks the child to his right if she will be ready to carry on this time. She is. The teacher reminds the children that they know lots of animals that they can say. But, if they get stuck they can show a thumbs-down to pass this time and have their turn another time.

First time around the circle the children say familiar animals; some add descriptive words, some add actions or sounds. The second time around the circle some children are extending the range and complexity of the descriptive words, more are adding actions or vocal sounds, one or two have chosen imaginary beasts, e.g. a fire-eating dragon, roar!

The opportunity for hearing the ideas of others and having some thinking time by having a number of turns has changed the imaginative quality of the children's responses.

With more vivid descriptions of their chosen animal, the children have real expressive intentions when choosing the timbre of the instrument which they will play their rhythm patterns on.

Songs

For a whole collection of brilliant ideas for using songs as a starting point for composition, look at the songbooks devised by Kaye Umansky. These include 'Bobby Shaftoe, Clap Your Hands' and 'Three Singing Pigs.' Using familiar melodies, Kaye has devised a mass of songs which either direct improvising or composing activies or lend themselves to reinterpretation. Most teachers could take this idea and create their own songs, for or with the children, to suit their own needs. Creating accompaniments for songs (as in Chapter 4) is another composing opportunity.

Pictures

CLASSROOM STORY
Every picture tells a story

Holly, a postgraduate trainee, was working with a Year 5/6 class. The focus of Holly's unit of work was 'How music is composed from a variety of stimuli', QCA unit 21.

In the first lesson the children had performed and composed using non-standard notation in the form of graphic symbols, very similar to those used in Chapter 4. Although the children met the learning objective, Holly felt that the stimulus had been rather abstract and not truly connected with the children's own experience. The children had not been composing for a real purpose. In the second lesson she changed her approach.

The learning objective for the second lesson was to create and perform a piece of music based on an image. The class had been studying *Charlie and the Chocolate Factory* in literacy. Using the interactive whiteboard, Holly showed the children a still image of the chocolate room from the original film. The class were excited by the image and they knew about that part of the story. The children had vivid ideas about what the characters might be feeling and could suggest ways in which these feelings might be expressed through music. They felt that the mood of the picture was exciting and magical. Holly asked them to bear this in mind in their group compositions. The children had plenty of ideas about instruments, melodies and rhythms. Having shared ideas as a class, the children were then free to create a piece of music. To create optimum conditions for children to be able to hear each other and focus on their group experimenting, Holly had organised additional space for the children to work in. Three groups worked in the classroom supported by Holly and three groups worked outside supervised by the TA. The children knew they had ten minutes to put their piece together and that Holly had high expectations of their performances. All groups were on task. They all created appropriate pieces of music. Most tried to create a magical and exciting atmosphere. The children had clear parameters to work within but the freedom for self-expression and creativity were still there.

The children performed some of their compositions in a *Charlie and Chocolate Factory* assembly. Teachers and other pupils were all very impressed. The children were really proud of their performance.

Moods

CLASSROOM STORY
Let's help mummy bear!

Sandra noticed how much her Year 1 class seemed to enjoy singing the action song 'Teddy bear, Teddy bear' which she had taught them. Because it only used the two notes g and e, all the children could sing it well. Sandra decided that giving the children the chance to play around with the notes g and e themselves on chime bars would be a good way to reinforce the learning. She also wondered if it might be a way for children to make up their own songs but she wasn't sure. The children were quite familiar with exploring sounds on the sound table and did this all the time. Sandra felt that they needed more of a challenge. This is what happened.

During circle time in the last half hour of the afternoon, Sandra's mobile phone went off. For a while she very obviously ignored it. The children told her that the phone was ringing, but Sandra insisted it couldn't be her phone, hers was switched off. Eventually, once every child had noticed what was going on, Sandra answered the phone. This was what the children heard.

Hello...Yes, it is Class One...Yes, this is the teacher...Of course we will help if we can, I'll just ask the children. Children, its Mrs Bear on the phone. She's got a problem that she thinks you could help with. Will you try? All the children are very keen to help. *I see...oh, dear...well,* we are all music composers in this class, *I'm sure we'll come up with lots of ideas.* It seemed that Barnaby Bear was having trouble getting to sleep at night, then in the morning he was having trouble waking up! Mrs Bear wondered if the children could compose some 'going to sleep' music and some 'waking up' music to help him. The next morning, there was a sleeping teddy bear in a bed on the music table, there were also three different pairs of chime bars g and e and a tape recorder.

Objects

Objects are concrete, tangible, holdable and may be even smellable. Stimuli which engage all the senses have a place in the musical composing repertoire. We have used the idea of creating rhythmic phrases from words in previous chapters. For young children, words may still be rather abstract materials. Using real objects which can be seen, pointed to and named in real time may be more appropriate.

Teaching example

The teacher has two dolls sitting at her feet. The children recognise the dolls from the television. They are Rosie and Jim. The children know that Rosie and Jim only talk when there is no one around, they are very shy. For this reason, the teacher asks the children if they will be the voices for Rosie and Jim and if they will say the characters' names when the teacher points to them. The teacher points to Jim and the children say, *Jim*. Keeping a slow and steady pulse, the teacher points to Jim four times and the children respond well, *Jim, Jim, Jim, Jim*. Then its Rosie's turn; the children notice that Rosie's name has two sounds whereas Jim's only has one. Still keeping a steady pulse, the teacher points to Rosie and Jim in combination, after a bit of hesitation the children chant the pattern, *Jim Jim Rosie, Rosie*. It is then just a small step to the children recognising pictures of Jim or Rosie and making the same response to them. This time the children not only say the names, but also have a go at clapping the names. In effect the children are becoming familiar symbols which represent one sound in the pulse space **I** (*Jim*, or tea as we have described it) or two equal sound in the pulse space **Π** (*Ro-sie*, or co-ffee).

Pentatonic scale

The pentatonic scale in C, *c d e g a*, can give all sorts of opportunities for composing. The scale itself is within most children's easily sung vocal range, it includes the natural interval that they sing instinctively. It is readily accessible on the tuned instruments to be found in most primary schools. Interestingly, when played against each other in parts or layers, the combinations of notes sound pleasing and harmonious to the ear. Clearly it is not helpful material for creating tense, angular, discordant music but useful for many other purposes. Children need lots of experiences in hearing, singing and playing the notes of the pentatonic scale in C. Many of the examples we have used for singing or playing have employed some of the notes in a limited way and this is a useful scaffolding structure.

Often the sequence will involve children becoming familiar with the *g* to *e* sound e.g. 'Teddy bear, teddy bear' (Appendix 3). The notes *a* and *c* are then included (if you sing or play the tune of 'Ring a ring a roses' starting on *g*, you will have a good example of this).

Children can be encouraged to make up phrases for copying games using the set of three adjacent notes, *c d e*, the two adjacent notes *g a*, and jumping over the gap from *g* down to *e*.

Teaching example

The class are arranged in a horseshoe shape in the hall. Pairs of children are sitting behind tuned instruments; glockenspiels, xylophones, metallophones and sets of chime bars.

Each child can see and reach their own set of notes, *c d e g a*. The teacher had already prepared the children to carefully remove the *f* and *b* keys before they left class.

The children have seen a series of dragon images on the interactive whiteboard. They have used talk partners to gather as much information about dragons as they could. They have collected and listed dragon features.

The teacher explains that there is a scale which is sometimes known as the dragon scale because of its special properties. Although many cultures use this scale to make folksongs and tunes, the sound feels rather oriental. The teacher plays the scale on her instrument and asks the children to listen and count how many notes. Five notes are heard. It is called the pentatonic scale because it has five notes. Five is a mystical number in some cultures. When the notes are sounded together they make a concordant sound, there are no clashes, a harmony. The teacher then asks the child nearest the piano to see if they can spot any set of five there. The black keys are arranged in fives a set of three and a set of two.

The teacher plays the first three notes of the scale on a tuned instrument singing and naming the notes *c d e* after she plays. The children sing the notes back. She then plays, names and sings *g* and *a*.

The class teacher then sings a song which matches the notes of the scale moving by step from the *c* to *a* for line 1 and from *a* to *c* for line two.

c   d   e g   a   a   a

Climb -ing up the dra -gon's tail

a   g   e   d c   c   c

Slid -ing down his shi -ny scales

The children listen to the song then sing back the tunes to the teacher. They then sing a second time showing the contour of the pitch using their hands. Finally, the teacher asks the children to play along on their instrument as they sing.

The teacher has taken some of the features which the children had listed about dragons and has made some accompanying phrases:

- fiery breath;
- massive flapping wings;
- ancient monster.

The children's task is to make up some mini tunes, some melodic ostinati, based on *c d e* for *massive flapping wings*, *g a* for *fiery breath* and any of the five notes for *ancient monster*. These will be the accompaniments for the song and could also be a way of turning the song into four parts.

Creative uses of music technology

Use of computer software

Loop-based programs

The most frequently used software uses so-called 'loops' which are essentially little musical phrases (melody, rhythm or sound) that can be repeated at will. They may be treated as ostinati or linked together with other phrases to make longer melodies. These include 'Compose', and 'Super duper looper'. The programs offer a range of possible loops which children can set out in tracks on a score. The loops of sound appear as distinctively coloured or patterned blocks which can be moved around on screen. Compose creates one track but Super dooper and others enable multi-tracking. The sounds available are chosen so that when combined they will harmonise. The children can make many choices about structure (beginnings, middles and ends) and how many tracks to combine and thus where to include 'windows' in the texture. This example builds up the layers initially, has a window halfway through with only one sound, and ends accumulatively with all the sounds together. This composer also decided to have one track, perhaps percussion, that runs throughout the piece.

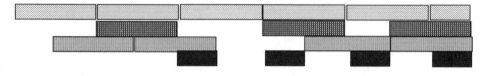

Drum machines

Children can combine rhythm tracks to create very exciting and satisfactory complex rhythms using programmes such as Toolkit, which is found within the 2 Simple software range. The advantage is that complex textures can be performed in ways that would be impossible acoustically because of the need for very sophisticated performance skill. These rhythms can be used to great effect in the background of acoustic performance.

Use of electric keyboards

It is important to remember that keyboards are part of music technology and they add to the range of possible sounds available to children. Also they provide some ready-made 'samples' of music such as rhythm patterns which can be incorporated into compositions.

Teaching example

A group of four children are creating a sequence of four rhythms derived from phrases to do with the sea, e.g. 'running on the sand' ⌐ ⌐ I Z (It is spoken to a count of 4 so the last beat is a rest.)

They choose hand-held percussion instruments to play the rhythms on and then run the sequence four times around. Finally they add a percussion accompaniment on an electric keyboard. This creates a varied rhythmic pattern with varied instrumental sounds against a constant rhythm and sound.

Reflecting on the composing process

In the composing classroom stories and teaching examples, you will have recognised teachers explicitly facilitating children's creativity. In the 'Jack and the Beanstalk' story, the teacher recounted to the child who played his 'climbing down the beanstalk idea', what he had actually done. Catching the composing process in action and encouraging children to explain the process is an important strategy for supporting children's understanding. In this way the teacher can help the children to reflect upon their compositions, understand how they went about achieving them in light of their intentions, and this naturally encourages the analytical process of making judgements and considering by what criteria we might do this.

CLASSROOM STORY
Making creative composing decisions explicit

Hajid wanted to give the children the chance to create their own compositions using a pulse grid. First the children practised the skills and understanding that they would need to make and play their own pieces.

1. The children joined Hajid in playing a pulse pattern: clap   clap   rest   rest
   Hajid encouraged the children to 'play' the rest as well as the sounds, an open hands gesture, to show that the pulse was still there. In turn around the circle each child said their name in the two-pulse rest space.
2. Hajid played some pulse patterns in 4 for the children to copy, using combinations of claps and rests:

clap	clap	rest	rest
clap	rest	clap	clap
clap	rest	rest	clap
clap	rest	rest	rest
clap	clap	rest	clap
rest	clap	clap	clap
rest	rest	clap	clap

   He asked the children to notice the patterns they found most tricky. It was when the rests came at the beginning of the set. Hajid then invited the children to suggest different body percussion to play, they chose stamping feet. It was quite hard to 'play' the rests with feet.
3. Finally Hajid asked if any of the children would like to lead the copying game. Georgia led her version using a head taps and James led his using a chest drum. Hajid was interested to know why they chose these sounds. Georgia thought head taps would be easy for everyone to see; she hadn't been able to see the feet patterns properly. James wanted everyone to look like Tarzan.

Hajid then showed the children an empty pulse grid in sets of four. He explained that each space represented a pulse and that he was going to compose a pattern for them to play using either a single sound in the space or no sound, a rest. Hajid then composed the first line and signed his initials to show it was his composition.

After a count of four he guided the children along the first line with his composer pen, showing the pulse, as the children clapped out the pattern. After congratulating the class on playing a very steady pulse and reading the grid accurately, Hajid asked for a child to compose the next line. David immediately offered, came up to the whiteboard and put the dots in for line 2 without any hesitation. After reminding him to sign his composition, Hajid asked David if he would lead the class in playing his line so that he could hear what it sounded like. He did. Hajid asked David how well the class had done. David replied they had played really well. Hajid then asked David to explain a bit more what he meant by playing well. David gave a really good analysis: *they all played together and they didn't play when it was a rest*. Shabana came next. She took a bit longer to put her pattern on the board. Having composed line 3 she led the class in her composition but wanted thigh slaps, not claps. Hajid asked Shabana if she had made any particular decisions when making up her pattern. She had just wanted something that was different from the other two lines. Last up was Liam. He took quite a while to decide on what to put, was looking at the other lines and seemed to be weighing something up. *Looks like you're thinking really carefully there, Liam*, encouraged Hajid. Liam composed line 4.

The class were not quite as accurate at playing Liam's line. They had to have a bit of practice, but they got it in the end. When Hajid asked Liam if he had a particular thing in mind, Liam replied that he had used lots of rests at the beginning because that's what eveyone thought was most tricky, but he wanted a sound at the end *to finish it off*.

●	●		●
●		●	
●			●
			●

Line 1
Hajid's model

Line 2
David understood the idea and applied it.

Line 3
Shabana understood the idea and made a particular decision based on analysis and intention.

Line 4
Liam had a complex idea based on a range of musical understandings and awareness.

Everyone got there, but what is important is how the children achieved this, what they were intending, as well as the teacher and how different individuals' success criteria would need to reflect this.

A SUMMARY OF **KEY POINTS**

> **You have thought about what it means to be a creative teacher and have considered the connections and distinctions between being creative in your teaching and teaching for the children's creativity.**

> **You have applied some of your understanding to a musical context, in particular to some of the ways in which you might stimulate and engage children in building their composing skills.**

What next?

The most important thing to take away from this chapter is the will and desire to have a go. Look out for creative teachers in your placements and talk with them and learn from them. Be open to new ideas and ways forward. Let children show you their ingenuity and inspire you to find alternative ways of teaching music. Seek out teachers who give children the opportunity to make up their own music and find out how they approach the task. Many schools will have visiting musicians who may be able to share their experiences of creating, improvising and composing music themselves and with children.

As with any other area of creative endeavour, composing can be an exhilarating experience. Children can gain a wonderful sense of achievement, in a unique and memorable way. But, as Glover reminds us, *exploration is a serious business. The spirit of exploration at best combines the driving sense of excitement at possibilities opening up ahead with the discipline of thorough investigation and observation of detail* (1994, p56).

Enjoy the journey!

REFERENCES REFERENCES **REFERENCES** REFERENCES **REFERENCES** REFERENCES

Corrie, C. (2004) *Becoming emotionally intelligent*. Stafford: Network Education Press.

Glover, J. and Ward, S. (1998) *Teaching music in the primary school*, 2nd edition. London: Cassell

Glover, J. and Young, S. (1999) *Primary music. Later years*. London: Falmer Press.

National Advisory Committee on Creative and Cultural Education (NACCCE) (1999) *All our futures: Creativity, culture and education* (The Robinson Report). London: DfEE

Nicholls, S. (1992) *Bobby Shaftoe, clap your hands – Musical fun with new songs from old favourites*. London: A & C Black

Nicholls, S. (1998) *Michael Finnigan, tap your chinigin – Developing music skills with new songs from old favourites*. London: A & C Black

Umansky, K. (1998a) *Three singing pigs*. London: A & C Black

Umansky, K. (1998b) *Three rapping rats – Making music with traditional stories*. London: A & C Black

6
Progression in children's musical learning

By the end of this chapter you should:

- **have some basic understanding of the musical development of children from birth to the end of the primary years;**
- **know what are the natural musical expressions of children at these ages;**
- **know some of the musical capabilities of children at different ages;**
- **have some strategies that meet the needs of children at specific ages.**

This chapter addresses the following Professional Standards for QTS:
Q1, Q7(a), Q14, Q18, Q22

Children's natural musical development

In order that you can plan appropriately for different age groups it will be useful to have some awareness of how children develop musically. There is folk wisdom about children's development in general and of the role music may play in their conceptual development. But it will be useful to place this in the context of research which, although it cannot establish absolute certainty, will bring us nearer to understanding.

From before birth children have awareness of sound and as mentioned in Chapter 3 as early as two days old can recognise the sound of their mother's voice (De Casper and Fifer, 1980) and make limited musical discriminations of timbre (O'Connel, 2003) within one week. It should not be surprising that this particular element is so significant early on since the very survival of the baby may depend on recognition of parents' voices. However, interestingly, the same infants are able to discriminate durational changes to tones and this indicates that awareness of rhythm also develops early in children. These functions grow as the auditory cortex grows. There is strong evidence that the brain produces many more synapses (neuronal connections) than will be required and then as some remain unused because of any lack of relevant stimulus they die away. The brain cavity is limited and hence cannot afford to retain unused capacity. Thus it is important that parents sing to their baby if the auditory functions of the brain are to develop. Clearly singing is the most significant musical activity at this early stage since a young child has limited ability to physically control the playing of instruments. Also, while learning to sing a melody can be largely intuitive, the ability to select and move around the keys of an instrument requires a higher level of conscious musical awareness.

RESEARCH SUMMARY RESEARCH SUMMARY RESEARCH SUMMARY RESEARCH SUMMARY

In these early developmental stages musical play is highly significant. The Pillsbury Study in the USA (1941/1978) was based on the premise that young children possess an innate musicality and that if allowed freedom to play in a potentially rich environment, they would display this musicality in a coherent form embedded in their general playful behaviours. The study was based on observation of children's activity in a nursery well equipped with musical instruments.

It was found that all young children are prodigious producers of a rich variety of spontaneous musical play and that there are some broad common features of this play. First was that these were overwhelmingly vocal but subsequent to the main study there were three recognisable categories identified by Littleton (1991):

- singing;
- playing with instruments and sound-makers;
- spontaneous movement to music.

Musical play takes the form of individual singing or instrumental playing and social inter-action. Typically you may hear chant-like repetitive singing of short, mixed, verbal and musical ideas. On the other hand, it may take the form of more introverted solitary free-flowing singing. Incorporated into these will be snatches of known songs which are added to or altered. In international studies, Sundin (1960/1998) and Bjørkvold (1989/1992) found that the chant form is associated with social play and there is continu-ity between this and playground musical games played by older children. In instrumental or sound-maker musical play there will be heard the same exploration of pattern. Young (2003) demonstrates that what may initially appear to be random in fact reflects the structure of the instrument or particular arm gestures. Hence bodily movement becomes significant in the production of musical patterns and typically children will synchronise singing with movement. They may dramatise their play with toys with improvised vocali-sations and act out role-plays with incorporated singing.

PRACTICAL TASK PRACTICAL TASK PRACTICAL TASK PRACTICAL TASK PRACTICAL TASK

Learning objective: To become informed about how music is part of the life of children in Early Years settings.

When in an Early Years setting, observe children at play and note when music has a place.

Listen for chanting, free-flowing singing and the incorporation of known songs. Try to detect when these are part of solitary or social play.

Note the extent to which the setting encourages other forms of musical play by the inclusion of musical instruments in the play areas or modelling by adult helpers.

One of the characteristics of such play is that it is intrinsically motivated and controlled by the players – the only rules are those imposed by the players themselves. Hence if teachers or assistants become over-intrusive and directive the play may close down (Marsh and Young, 2006). The tension we need to recognise here is that in the Early Years there is continuity between the children's own spontaneous play and teacher-structured activity. There are means by which teachers influence the play in order to encourage particular forms of development. For instance, you may see a sound table set out to encourage the use of particular instruments.

Musical play does continue into the junior years but is most clearly evident in the play-ground. It becomes merged with the oral tradition associated with school break times and thus deliberately separated from teacher-led activity. Although playground game songs have traditional foundations they are subject to the same improvised variations and continual change to which earlier forms of play are subject. Thus it is that songs vary in their words from region to region. The sharing of new ideas or variations promotes collaboration and cohesiveness within friendship groups. Interesting manifestations of this in more recent times are the evidence of the similar songs in different parts of the world. A song heard in Los Angeles, USA, *Say, say my play-mate* becomes *See, see my play-mate* in Sydney, Australia, with a tune that has the same contour but uses a more limited note range. Frequently there will be the introduction of parts of pop songs; for example, the song *Down, down baby* is derived from a 1960s pop song *Shimmy shimmy Kokopop*. Spice Girls songs became popular songs for developing dance routines in playgrounds but such routines may also be accompanied by improvised clapping routines (Opie and Opie, 1988; Grudgeon, 2001). The song 'Barbie Girl' by Aqua became a clapping game in east London in 1997:

> I'm a Barbie girl, in a Barbie world
> Say goodbye, never cry
> Thanks for meeting you, bye bye.

The discussion of these features here is not just as a matter of background interest but because they provide evidence of the musical development of children as demonstrated spontaneously in their play. Also there are indications of what children find captivating, intriguing and satisfying in music, and knowledge of this is clearly important to teachers in their planning. There are two significant cautions to consider. Firstly that what has been described above is largely a girls' culture, as evidenced by the popularity of the Spice Girls dance routines in the early 2000s; and secondly that teachers need to consider carefully where to draw the line between acknowledging where children are developmentally and where they want to take them to through music education.

Issues relating to Early Years

The relationship of movement to music

The importance of relating movement to music in the Early Years cannot be overemphasised. Pugh and Pugh relate a very telling story of a three-year-old child being drawn into a street performance by a jazz band such that the dance to the music she began grows into movements that the players begin to respond to themselves. The initial sweeping movements become spikey movements and the band play in a correspondingly jerky manner (1998, p74). The same correspondence between gesture and musical character was explored in the passage about responding to recorded music through mark-making in Chapter 2 and will be in the section of Chapter 7 about art and music.

The relationship has long been recognised, particularly in those who take an interest in traditional music. The relationship between music and dance in some African traditions is so close that there is no word for music alone. In Europe the work of Jaques Dalcroze has been influential. Dutoit describes 'The method' of Dalcroze as *a series of varied exercises performed mostly to improvised music...This results in...[the body] expressing great music in movement – movement evoked by that music* (1965). Dalcroze perceived that the appreciation of music was a physical response that has become intellectualised. Often this physicality is still expressed in nodding heads and tapping feet or wide arm gestures. The French conductor Ernest Ansermet wrote in 1924: [Jaques Dalcroze] *made use of the sense...called the rhythmic muscular sense, transforming the phenomenon of time into that of space*. In contemporary language we would speak of the 'kinaesthetic' sense.

The work developed in the 1920s and 1930s by Ann Driver encouraging expressive movement by children in response to music clearly drew on the idea that music has a bodily analogy (1936). This approach became known as 'Music and Movement' and in the post-war years the BBC took a leading role in promoting the work in its schools' broadcasts.

The conventions of Early Years music education have embedded these principles in everyday practice but perhaps it has not always been understood why they are important. This can be answered by looking at the research that supports what has been understood intuitively. The work of Piaget and Bruner (Beard, 1969; Lawton, 1973) emphasise the principle of working from the concrete, or in Bruner's words, the enactive, stage to the abstract. Music educators have also taken up this theme. Carl Orff integrated dance into his creative music schemes by establishing accompanying dance as one of the main purposes of music composition (Keetman, 1974). Kodaly used hand gestures to provide a visual representation of pitch. Kemp's research findings (1990) have shown that musical memories are not confined to sound but record the gestures associated with the sound. Thus the sound of a cymbal will be remembered as a sweeping gesture of the right hand and the sensation of vibration in the left as well as the crash.

Developing pulse and tempo through movement

Children do need a variety of experiences or the opportunity to respond in their own way to the pulse of music. The whole-class directed activities to be seen in the final section of this chapter should be complemented by either encouragement to respond differently or by presenting a good range of activities. Some children will find marching in time difficult but will be able to rock a doll in their arms to the pulse of a lullaby. Other forms of timekeeping could include tapping hands on knees, nodding heads or tapping an instrument (especially one secured to a stand).

When leading a song with actions it is worth spending time drawing attention to the actions. For instance, you may see some children following the rhythm of the words rather than the pulse. You can draw attention to a child who is following the pulse particularly well and ask the class to follow the actions of that child. In the song 'Wind the bobbin up' the actions will tend to follow the rhythm of the song, as in:

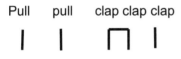

Pull   pull   clap clap clap

However, a song such as 'Down by the station, early in the morning' will be accompanied by a regular steam engine gesture by the arms to the pulse of the song.

It will be a good idea to choose songs with different tempi so that the children are used to keeping slow as well as fast beats. A nursery rhyme such as 'Hickory Dickory Dock' could have one group *tick-tocking* with a finger and another tapping on knees and if children are a little more experienced in Key Stage 1 one could be playing the *tick tock* on wood blocks.

Developing pitch through movement

In Chapter 1 when we introduced the element of pitch we used the example of a teacher pretending to clasp a note in her hand and as she moved it up and down encouraged the children to shift the note they sang up and down. A development of this could be that the children move their own hands up and down and begin to strongly associate high notes with high up in space. It could be a toy being taken for a journey up the stairs along a corridor and down a lift, perhaps. Such stories can be pictured on sheets for children to work with independently.

The children can have a hand held horizontally in front of them. This can move to a 'high' position and back down again with the following song. The two high and low pitches are indicated at the beginning of the lines.

g	Up	up and	up to the sky and
e	down	down	down to the ground

Any hand movement that indicates the rise and fall of music will help children to differentiate pitch more clearly. When introducing a new song it is a good idea with all ages to follow the pitch of the song with appropriate hand gestures if you feel reasonably secure about where the pitches rise and fall.

Should young children learn notation?

From our point of view the answer depends on how we interpret Early Years. If we take the curriculum definition the period is up to and including the Reception class then we would say no. However, for convenience, sometimes Key Stage 1 is included in the Early Years and what we have written about children's use of early forms of notation will certainly apply to Key Stage 1. We have taken a stance that follows the implications of the National Curriculum which suggests some teaching of graphic notation systems but also we have acknowledged that learning to use notation will be necessary if children wish to learn Western orchestral or band instruments. It can be seen as something that could be learnt when needed. Therefore the motivation to read music lies in the desire to learn an instrument. We would suggest that wholesale music notation teaching to any primary children will be more of a hindrance to becoming musical because it will take away valuable time that can be used to experience actual music. Suzuki (1969), the violin teacher, advocated that children should learn to play by ear in the early stages just as children learn language from the adults around them. He enabled young players to play the music they heard in their heads rather than to react to symbols on a page. He argued that young children are not experienced enough to be able to relate the symbols to truly musical sounds.

We would argue that children at Key Stage 1 certainly can benefit from some simple graphic notation systems so long as they have had substantial music experience to relate it to.

Classroom organisation in the Early Years

Music is part of the nursery school environment. Sometimes it will be recorded music in the background or used to accompany activities. It may be on audio CD or tape ready for children to listen to. It may be in the form of instruments set out in a quiet corner for children to use as part of their continuous provision. There will be some formal whole group singing and musical activity.

REFLECTIVE TASK

Learning objective: To reflect on how to structure musical activity as continuous provision.

Consider how a set of four instruments could be set out so that the children would compare their timbres. How much could be left to the children to decide for themselves? What could the teacher do to prepare the children?

The Early Years curriculum

Music falls within the creative development section of practice guidance for the Early Years Foundation Stage. It is interesting to note the concern about how to nurture creativity in children in the Early Years. It is recognised that teachers should be making an enabling environment in which *creativity, originality and expressiveness are valued* (DfES, 2007, p105). There is value given to relationships that ensure children feel secure to have a go and feel adventurous and that planning gives time for children to work through their ideas to a satisfactory finish.

The music curriculum for children approaching Reception age gives emphasis to singing but also to moving to music through ring games and tapping out rhythms. It also draws attention to the fact that children at this age will enjoy singing to themselves and be able to make up songs.

There is a recognisable shift in the curriculum for children of Reception age. Teachers are encouraged to give children opportunities to play instruments and to explore timbre in order to express feelings and ideas. The awareness of pattern and the ways movement can be matched to music link with mathematical understanding at this stage. The children begin to have a memory for a range of songs.

Within the notes for this stage there is also some guidance given about inclusiveness in the arts in general through awareness of different cultural traditions or disabilities and how this may impact on children's capacity, approach or willingness to participate.

Issues relating to later years

Boys and music

The description of playground musical play implies that girls have a play culture that already sets them up to find music intrinsically enjoyable. So you need to consider carefully how boys may be fully engaged by music in school. There is research evidence to show that boys are more extrinsically motivated than girls in general (Renwick and McPhearson, 2006) but that younger children of both sexes are more intrinsically motivated by activities than older children. Hence younger children of both sexes will respond to the intrinsically enjoyable aspect of a musical activity and the stronger this is, the more divorced they will be from any other counter-factors. As they grow into the final years of the primary school, social factors and considerations of utility may become more significant. What a child may consider to be lost by engaging in the activity will be more carefully weighed up. Thus the personal prestige a musical activity itself and particularly the success it brings to the individual may become critical. Social relationships become much more significant. Does musical activity take the child away from socially important activities such as games, perhaps? In the final two years of primary school both boys and girls need to begin to establish their gender identity. Boys will ask themselves, what is boyish musical activity? They may make, what seems to us to be, arbitrary choices on the basis of what is seen by themselves as asserting their identity as a boy.

REFLECTIVE TASK

Learning objective: To gather ideas about motivation and to evaluate relevant strategies.

What extrinsic motivations could you use to encourage full engagement in music by boys?

- Consider the timing of music activity so that it is not seen to be in competition with other activities that have a high value for the boys you are working with.

- Consider the strategies you have observed or tried yourself in other curriculum areas, such as particular groupings, opportunities for taking a lead and competition.

- Does giving rewards have a place here or at all?

You need to consider levels of motivation at different stages of development and hence how you may overcome any disincentives boys may feel.

In addition, boys will be found to respond particularly well to physical or kinaesthetic activity, however small a part that it may play in the learning experience. Adding movement to a performance will appeal to all children of course but remember not to make the routines too complicated. It is important to keep all children comfortably included. A simple example would be a group standing to one side of the classroom providing the 'body' percussion accompaniment to a rap chant. It need be no more than 'clap, clap stamp (left), stamp (right)' repeated as an ostinato. Dramatising a performance can add very greatly to the effect and the business of moving about eases the constraints of sitting in set positions.

Teaching example

The song 'Tongo' (a Polynesian canoeing song) which is sung in two simple parts, once learnt, can be performed by two groups facing each other across the classroom as if singing across the sea between two Pacific islands.

The teacher leads with Part 1 and signals to the class to sing Part 2 exactly echoing what she has sung.

She encourages the class to hold onto the last note of each phrase to the end of her own phrase so that the parts together create simple harmony.

She divides the class into two groups and positions them facing each other. One group then sings 1 and the other 2.

The physical movement involved in playing drums has a particular appeal to many boys. Also it is a good complementary activity to singing. It is worth collecting even the simplest of drums, such as those mentioned in Chapter 3 (plastic bins and large pots), in order to make a whole-class drumming activity possible.

CLASSROOM STORY
Rhythms in action

David's Year 6 class had been chanting, playing and composing patterns in four using 'teas', 'coffees' and rests. To inspire the children and provide an exciting context for applying their new skills and understandings David decided to create with the children a rhythm piece based around the timbres of African music, using particularly drums, rattles and metal cowbells. The children had listened and improvised along to a drumming track by Ben Badoo. David booked the hall for the lesson and had a circle of chairs ready with an extended collection of instruments in the centre.

David had already introduced the children to a children's rhyme that included combinations of known rhythms.

Pulse in 4	x	x	x	x				
	Up	like a	rock - et	-	Ι	Π	Π	Z
	Down	like the	rain	-	Ι	Π	Ι	Z
	Round	and	round	like a	Ι	Ι	Ι	Π
	Rail	- way	train	-	Ι	Ι	Ι	Z

Standing in a circle and chanting the rhyme, the children reached up for line one; crouched down for line two then marched in a circle to the pulse of lines three and four. This helped the children to physically feel the pulse in its metre of four and to gain a sense of each of the phrases.

David then chanted each line individually, clapping the syllables of the words as he spoke them. The children copied as an echo, saying and clapping the patterns.

In the centre of the circle David had collected groups of African-inspired instruments of different timbres. He had researched the school's resources and had supplemented these with a pair of congas, four djembe drums (two small/two medium), a range of different sized shekere and a two-tone metal agogo from his local music service.

The instruments were grouped as follows:

Group 1   Pair of congas, two medium djembe
Group 2   Small skinned instruments, a combination of tambourines and tambours
Group 3   Rattles, including the shekere
Group 4   Metal instruments including tin cans, pan lids, cowbells and the metal agogo
Group 5   Larger skinned instruments, including the small djembe

David divided the children into five groups and gave them a little time to explore the sounds of the instruments in each group. After the children had undertaken some free exploration he asked them to try out each of the four rhythms on their group of instruments and to be ready to say which pattern they found easiest to play.

To underpin the chance of success when putting all of the parts together David intended that group 1 would be playing the pulse to keep everyone together. To create variety, he reminded the children of the exploration they had previously done to find the liveliest part of the drum skin, and also reminded the children that they could play an open, ringing-out

---

sound on the drum with a cupped, bouncy hand or a closed, dull sound with a flat, then static hand (see Figure 4.1 on page 53).

As skills practice for everyone David asked the children to return to the circle of chairs and to turn their chairs round to face them. The children then made the shape of a capital T with their two hands on the sets of the chairs. The top of the T would be playing in the centre of the drum skin, the stem hand would be playing towards the edge where the lively place was. After a few minutes of free play using left or right hand at the top of the T and playing their chairs, a formal pattern was created as a variation of timbre for the pulse pattern in 4. The first beat was played with a closed sound in the centre of the chair's seat with the top of the T, the other three beats with an open sound towards the edge of the seat with the stem of the T.

Each group was then asked which part they had found easiest to play on their group of instruments. After some discussion, with children demonstrating the playing of the patterns, the following parts were decided upon:

Group 1   The pulse   *closed open open open*
Group 2   Line 1 of the rhyme
Group 3   Line 2 of the rhyme
Group 4   Line 3 of the rhyme
Group 5   Line 4 of the rhyme, in the pattern *open, open, closed*.

The children returned to the centre of the circle and their group of instruments. After each group had practised their part, David encouraged the players to play one after the other. Group 1 played a steady pulse of four, after David's steady count in. Each group said and played their part of the rhyme one after the other. David encouraged the children to notice any areas that needed practice. The children spotted that each group had to be ready to come in straight after the group before had finished, with no gaps. The children also noticed that with each new entry the piece was getting faster. David praised the children for their careful appraisal and asked how they could overcome the problem. The children suggested that Group 1 should play all the way through to keep everyone together. David took the children's suggestion on board and the class then built the piece up in layers. First Group 1 set a steady count (metre) of four to the tempo of David's count; each group then came in and kept repeating their part until they saw the signal to stop.

As a final stage David played to the children an aural stop signal, on a cowbell. The first signal was played to the rhythm of the words 'Ready to stop'. When the children heard this they knew this was a warning that they would stop playing soon. The second time the signal was played the children needed to stop. Great fun was had as David tried to catch the children out with the stopping signals.

The culmination of all the children's hard work came in the afternoon when David had arranged that the class would play their new piece to Year 4, who were exploring Africa as a cross-curricular topic. David had a video of the performance made to show to colleagues in the music service how the children had used the welcome resources that David had borrowed. The video later became a star feature at Year 6 parents evenings.

General motivation in music

It will be useful to think about how children's motivation is affected by their self-concept. You also need to consider the relationship between this motivation and how realistic the goals are that they themselves or teachers set. In the Early Years they will often have unrealistic images of themselves and portray their abilities in broad terms, e.g. *I'm good at school*. In the later primary years children begin to be able define the concept of themselves as learners in more discriminating ways (Marsh, 1990). They will be able to acknowledge weakness in one area, e.g. *I'm bad at drawing*, while being confident to assert competence in another area, e.g. *I'm a good speller*. They may become more careful in the way they help to maintain their self-concept by avoiding fully participating in activities, withholding effort, choosing easy tasks and questioning the value of the activity (Anderman et al., 1999). Because there is such a close link between self-concept and achievement, researchers take different lines on whether time should be spent on raising self-image prior to engaging in the challenge or spend time helping children to develop better learning strategies (Marsh, 1984). Clearly both are important and have a dynamic relationship. However, this relationship is one that needs to be carefully considered in a subject such as music in which children's accomplishments are made very public both at a smaller scale, working in groups or in class, and more challengingly in a school assembly. These public forums for performance display ability differences that children in the final two years of primary school are increasingly aware of. Self-concepts are increasingly informed by such events as evidenced by tearful upsets or occasional resistance to participate fully.

REFLECTIVE TASK

Learning objective: To have strategies in place that will ensure children's performances are positive experiences.

There are clear benefits derived from performance in music and these have implications for non-music subjects that don't usually present opportunities for public recognition. However, on the other hand, the public nature of all the arts either through performance or display does present a problem for teachers if children's self-concepts are negatively influenced.

How can you minimise the negative effects of performance in your music lessons? Or, how can you give emphasis to the positive aspects of performance?

The status that music has in society, as reflected in school, informs the importance that boys and girls give to the activity. There may be some for whom music is largely an extra-curricular activity and their motivation is also driven by success in external music-making or by the status musical activity is given at home.

CLASSROOM STORY

Samantha, a final year music specialist BA primary education student in her Year 3 placement, had noticed Year 3 boys showing some 'embarrassment' in music lessons. She anticipated that in her following placement in a Year 6 class she would meet this again and possibly more so. However, she found that many of the boys were very outgoing in music lessons and were not afraid to sing and dance in front of the rest of the class or indeed the school. She questioned her preconceptions: are there gender differences or are responses simply individual? She discovered that the school in which she was placed is well known in the area for the quality of its dramatic productions and that the boys had a strong role in these shows. Also, and this may be particularly significant, one of the boys had taken a lead role in a major film. The boys were clearly responding to a positive role model and to a school ethos that supported their full engagement in music.

The decline in self-concept in relation to music during this developmental phase in Western societies is general and this is attributed by Wigfield et al. (1997) to children's beliefs about the importance of music. However, it is evident that children in Western societies do associate musical competence with technical skills which they have only in part. This should not surprise us when musical skills are so publicly displayed in the media, whether in pop or classical form. At this stage children are beginning to see, and hear, very plainly the gap between what they can do and what adults can do. In other subjects this is not as plain to see. Children do not compare their ability in geography or RE with adults; there are no models against which to make the comparison.

Bearing all of this in mind, we need to be clear that what could to some appear to be a disincentive, to others may be seen as a model to emulate. Those children who are secure about their own musical ability will respond well to a teacher modelling playing an instrument either in the classroom or in assembly. Hence it is very important to set realistic and achievable goals that are seen as relevant and worthwhile to these children. This is what will maintain a positive self-concept and hence receptiveness to good musical models and challenges.

PRACTICAL TASK PRACTICAL TASK PRACTICAL TASK PRACTICAL TASK PRACTICAL TASK

Learning objective: To be able to create realistic and achievable musical goals.

Design an activity for a group of four children (Year 3/4), making use of six 'rhythm cards' which results in a composition to be performed by the group. (See the 'Progression in duration' section at the end of this chapter for ideas about how to introduce these cards.) Consider how the cards can be used to make a graphic score as part of the task. There should be at least two stages to the activity which represent interim goals.

The extra requirements of the Key Stage 2 Curriculum

Singing

The implications at Key Stage 2 that children should *sing songs* in…*two parts, with clear diction, control of pitch, a sense of phrase and musical expression* can be quite a challenge to generalist teachers with little or no training in music. However, some simple guidance will, we hope, dispel these fears to some extent.

By the junior stage children's voices are taking on new characteristics. The initial range of five or six notes *d* to *a* that is the comfortable range for pre-school and early Key Stage 1 children, as set out in Chapter 3, becomes extended. However, the extent of that extra range is determined by experience. The comfortable range for some children will be high and hence they will have no difficulty reaching upwards to high *d*, *e* and *f* and for some with choir experience higher still. Others will find they are more comfortable in the deeper range; from middle *c* down to *B*, *A* and even *G*. Boys in the upper Key Stage 2 period may feel that to assert their boyishness they should sing low in their register when in fact their natural voice is perhaps higher. It is true that girls do have an extra top range to their voices in the pre-pubertal period that boys do not naturally have but differences are very slight and boys can be trained to sing in that top range and produce very beautiful sounds as evidenced by trebles in cathedral choirs. So the general advice is to respond to children's natural abilities, interests and enthusiasms and to downplay misconceptions based on social pressures.

Children in the junior years have a very great capacity to respond to challenges. This is the stage at which children will respond enthusiastically to the teacher who enthuses her class by setting targets as modest as *Let's sing our song to the next door class or the school at Friday assembly*. Such motivations will energise the class and give extra purpose to singing lessons. These children can memorise extraordinary amounts of lyrics in a short time, so do encourage learning words and singing without prompts. This will produce a better, more focused, sound. Varying the form of performance will add interest and meaning to singing for children of this age. Semi-dramatisation in the positioning of the singers helps to bring a song to life and to give it expression (see also Chapter 8).

These children will respond to the disciplines of making sure their audience can hear the words. Games of saying tongue twisters slowly and then fast will add fun to the activity. A tongue twister such as *Lotty licks lollies lolling in the lobby* will ensure the tongues of the singers are fully engaged. Alternatively,

> *Betty Botter bought some butter,*
> *But she said the butter's bitter.*
> *If I put it in my batter,*
> *It will make my batter bitter*

will exercise the lips.

Encourage the consonants at ends of words as well as beginnings by telling the children to count the length of a note in their head and place the final consonant precisely. This is another skill to be mastered and when set as a challenge they will respond. Try directing the singing of long notes on words such as 'went' to different counts to see if all the members of the group can make the final 'nt' sound at the same time or even plan for different groups to end at different times for a special effect.

Part songs and chants

Two-part singing is another way of adding interest and drama to a song. The simplest forms are simple chant and if there is some humour as well, it goes down well with this age group.

The shark (traditional) (in *Banana Splits* collected by Anna Sanderson)
One group (2) have an ostinato chant: Doo –doo, doo bedee doo,
The other group (1) tell the story:

Group 1   There was a boy,
There was a girl
They went for a swim
A swim in the sea
They took off their clothes
All of their clothes
They swam so far
Really far
There was no one around
Just no one around
Totally empty
Except for the sharks!   Voice 2 change to 'Na-na na na na na'
Daddy shark
Mummy shark
Granpa shark
Baby shark   Voice 2 change to 'Wee–wee,wee wee wee wee'
They swam so fast   Voice 2 change back to 'Doo-doo', etc.
Really fast
To the shore
Out of the water
Ran so fast
Really fast
Totally empty
Except for the sharks!

Rounds

Rounds are the most common form of two-part singing. They are very versatile. Firstly, they can be simply sung altogether as a straight song. However, the performance would be very short if it was not repeated. So it is worth having different kinds of performance for each repetition: solos or groups, quiet or loud and so on.

Secondly, the teacher may take the first phrase and treat this as an ostinato for a small group while the main group sing the song right through.

Then it may be sung as a round in two or more parts. If the children's voices are not very well in tune, it is better not to have more than two parts.

Teaching example

Now I walk in beauty (native American)

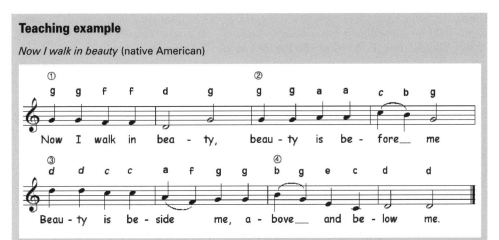

This song works well as a chant but if sung as a round the class is split into two. Group one begins and then when they get to figure 2 the second group begin. Children in later primary years will enjoy the whole body movement with this song.

The singers stand in a circle.
At 1 they stand with hands to the side
At 2 they gesture to before them with their right hand
At 3 they gesture to the right side
At 4 they gesture up and down.

Appraising

There is the additional requirement (marked in italics) in the National Curriculum at Key Stage 2 for children to:

a) *analyse and compare sounds;*
b) explore and *explain* their own ideas and feelings about music using movement, dance, *expressive language* and musical vocabulary;
c) improve their own *and other's work in relation to its intended effect.*

This is part of the requirement to 'appraise', a component of the curriculum that has been neglected in the past but is familiar as a significant aspect of other subjects as evaluation. In order for this to work we have to by-pass or overcome the natural resistance to an analytical approach to the arts. Children and people in general may resist the idea of pulling apart an experience that they wish to feel in an intuitive and spontaneous way. However, when children compose they use the same thinking or analytical processes but use them in reverse, as it were. They respond to the challenge of thinking about putting together a composition. In the composing activities that you read about in Chapter 5 children had to make decisions and select from a range of options to maximise a particular effect they wanted to achieve. When appraising analytically we encourage children to be aware of those decisions and to speculate about what others may have considered. When works of art are familiar they take on a permanence and solidity that may deny us the possibility of imagining them half finished. Writers and film makers do sometimes play with their audiences by offering more than one possible ending or story line. It is precisely this way of thinking that we can encourage children to adopt. So, what might this look like in a classroom? In Chapter 2 you read an example about children appraising a musical conversation. This was a typical Key Stage 1 activity. At Key Stage 2 it might develop into the following.

Teaching example

Pairs of children are playing tuned percussion instruments. The notes f and b have been removed so that the instruments have only the notes of the pentatonic scale (c d e g a) on them. The first player plays a phrase of about four or five notes on the lower half of the instrument and the other creates an answering phrase. They improvise ideas for a period of five minutes, after which time the teacher asks one or two pairs to demonstrate to the rest of the class. The teacher then wants to guide the children to have particular plans in mind when creating responding phrases so she asks the children, *Was the answering phrase an echo, was it completely different or was it similar?* The children are being challenged to listen to the shape of the phrases they create. They may see that an answering phrase has the same rhythm as the question phrase but not the same notes. The beginning may be the same but not the end, and so on. She then encourages the children to develop three question and answer phrases that have these characteristics. They rehearse the questions and answers so that they are memorised and there is a shift from improvisation to composition.

(I have used the word 'phrase' because technically that is correct but the word 'tune' might well be used. It would be best, however, to speak of both phrases together making a tune.)

As we saw in Chapter 2, the idea of appraising may also apply to listening to recorded music. When children are younger this may be a very spontaneous process. They may feel an appropriate way of moving to a piece of music; heavy/light, fast/slow, smooth/ragged and through this to explore and explain their own ideas and feelings about music. As children mature, music begins to take on associations. For instance, some styles may be linked to advertising. It is interesting how loud and slow choral music has taken on sinister connotations; melodious and comforting sounds conjure up flying; and 'drum and bass' goes with youth in the advertising world. Working in a cross-curricular manner will enable children to find different musical vocabularies with which to articulate their feelings.

Learning objective: To experience an alternative way of responding to recorded music.

Roll out a piece of lining paper (one metre) and have large brushes and a range of colours and/or chalks to hand.

Choose two contrasting pieces of music to play over a period of about 15 minutes. As the first piece plays, respond to the rhythms that stand out. Draw with the brush or chalks different qualities of line according to the quality of the music, be it jagged, smooth or rolling. The lines should overlap and run off the edge of the paper. Then put on the second piece of music and choose colours according to the mood of the music and use these to fill in the gaps between the lines.

In doing this you will have become aware of rhythmic qualities in the music and the prevailing mood that music can so powerfully evoke. Now it will not be difficult to design a lesson for children along the same lines – you may need to use the hall.

The above practical task asks for total absorption in the music. This is a state of mind which we hope all can experience when drawn into activity such that the child loses a sense of the outside world. The term 'flow' has been associated with this state of mind when applied to a child's full application to a task (Csikszentmihalyi, 1990).

However, appraisal may take place when children are in a more detached state of mind. For instance, older children are able to make judgements about their own performance. Once they can move on from learning the notes or the words children may be encouraged to try out different ways of performing a verse of a song. A simple song such as 'Train is a coming' lends itself to variety between verses.

Learning objective: To be able to create variety in a performance through appraisal, with reference to 'improving their own and others' work in relation to its intended effect'.

Try this out with children in your next placement. Teach the song to the children and then ask the questions, 'How can we change our performance?' or 'How can we make our performance better?' How can these be expressed in child-friendly language?

This is a very simple song to learn:

If this first verse is sung neither quietly nor loudly (dynamics) and at a moderate speed (tempo), then you need to think about how to sing verse two differently:

Train is a-slowing, oh yeah

Then the next verse might change speed as it goes along:

Train is a-stopping, oh yeah

After, 'Better buy a ticket, oh yeah', there is an accelerating verse:

Train's getting faster, oh yeah

and after that you can make up your own verses.

Think about the kind of instrumental accompaniment that children of this age are capable of making. This is a one-chord (C) song in pentatonic notes so that you could draw on ideas from Chapter 4.

Progression in duration

To illustrate how musical skills, knowledge and understanding may develop throughout the primary years, I will set out an outline of progression in the element duration.

The word 'duration' is often misleading in that its components are much more familiar terms, e.g. rhythm and pulse. It is the umbrella term that is used in the National Curriculum and so we need to be familiar with it. However, in the Early Years the words used may need to be closer to home. 'Pattern' is useful because it makes the connection with other areas of work. Although the term 'beat' may be commonly used 'pulse' is a simple word and the concept straightforward. So it is with pulse that we will make a start.

Developing a sense of pulse

You will have gathered how important the link between music and movement must be in the early stages of teaching music. Action rhymes and songs with movement help to give meaning to the words but most importantly they will make the underlying pulse of the song visual and physically felt to the children. In music and movement lessons the children will be directed to move around the room in a manner that reflects the character of the music. Some aspects of this will be to do with dynamics and pitch of the music but most significant will be the tempo of the pulse. Gradually children will learn how to move in time to the pulse, especially if that pulse is heard very clearly as it is in dance music. In the following example the children may move in different kinds of ways but still with a military step.

Playing on the trumpet, we are
playing on the trumpet,
Playing on the trumpet in the
big brass band.

Playing on the horn, we are
playing on the horn,
Playing on the horn in the
big brass band.

When the children are a little older they may be more aware of their own pulse. This awareness may coincide with work on the human body in science. A short exercise in feeling the pulse is useful. One way of doing this is to ask all the children to find their pulse at the wrist and to tap their toe very quietly in time with the pulse. When the tempo is established, ask the children to tap louder and to try to keep their pulse distinct from others. Leading on from that in a way that keeps holding the pulse strongly kinaesthetic is to have the children standing in pairs one behind the other. The front children sing 'The Grand Old Duke of York' to the pulse which the children behind tap on their shoulders. The child in front should try to keep to the pulse the child behind is tapping regardless of whether it is in time with others in the class.

In Year 2 children will be able to take a leading role in being 'time-keepers'. This role is rather similar to the conductor or the drummer in a band. One child may have a two-tone wood block and play in time to marching on the spot. If the child finds it easier she or he may march around in a small circle. The marching pattern will help to regulate the pulse because it is actually quite difficult to walk or march in an irregular pattern.

At Key Stage 2, call-and-response activities such as 'Follow me', mentioned in Chapters 1 and 2, will exercise pulse-keeping by requiring children to make varied patterns while keeping the pulse regular. A variation of that activity is 'Switch' (Baxter, 1978) in which the teacher leads with a body sound to a regular pulse and the children copy. The teacher then changes to a new sound but tells the children not to change until they hear the word 'switch'. This means that at some moments the children will be making a different pattern to the teacher, which adds a level of complexity and challenge to keeping the pulse.

Long and short sounds

In the Early Years it is worth spending some time raising awareness of how rhythm is made up of long and short sounds and that these are formed into patterns.

To begin with, the teacher could play a cymbal and tell the children to stand up when the sound dies away. Then if the children are seated in a circle, different kinds of sound can be passed around. The shortest sounds will be passed very quickly and will flow round the group very fast. If all the children hold an instrument and each child has to wait until the sound of the one before them disappears before playing, a wonderfully random pattern of shorts and longs will be created. If a keyboard sound or blown instrument is included, the children's attention can be drawn to the difference between sounds that decay rapidly, like a wood block; sounds that resonate but still die away, like a cymbal; and a sustained sound like that from a keyboard.

The randomness of the last activity with instruments is a useful quality to remind children about when as they grow up and begin to assume that all music has to have a dominant beat to it. To extend this by linking music-making to drama can be useful. A teacher might ask the same children to create the sounds of dawn breaking by sitting silently in their circle and at some point one of them unprompted by the teacher to play a very quiet sound and then for others to follow, allowing intervals of silence in between.

Having explored longs and shorts in general and unpatterned sounds, we will look at more specific patterns of sounds and matching these to a pulse. A good way of making a start is to set up opportunities for children to have musical conversations with instruments. From Reception age upwards children are able to do this. The children may create free-flowing musical conversations or one child may simply echo the other. In between these two, and well suited to older children, would be the attempt of the second child to provide an 'answer' to the first child's 'question'. This might be a variation on the question in that most of it is the same but the ending is different or the reverse, as in this example.

Question: ᓭᓭᓭ ᓭᓭᓭ | | |

Answer: ᓭᓭ ∏ ᓭᓭ ∏ | | |

I have used the Kodály notation to help explain the point but would not use the formal notation until the children had experienced an intermediary stage.

A useful activity at this stage is to ask children to introduce symbols to indicate the kinds of sounds they are making, in effect a simple graphic score, so that someone else could by reading it recreate the original performance. The progression has been from the concrete, aural experience of music towards the more abstract symbols. An in-between stage could well be the use of little pictograms to indicate sounds so that there is not too big a leap into the use of abstract symbols. However, as children are getting used to written and numerical symbols at the stage, we are introducing the musical equivalent.

The teacher might then create a simple graphic score for the children to interpret, first of all for one instrument then for two or more at the same time.

PRACTICAL TASK PRACTICAL TASK PRACTICAL TASK PRACTICAL TASK PRACTICAL TASK

Learning objective: To develop skills in using and interpreting a simple graphic score system.

Interpret this single instrument score in a spontaneous way.

You will probably have played one tap on the triangles and left a one- or two-beat rest where there was a gap. Towards the end a sense of a metre of three may have emerged. Now try the following score but this time you need a partner. In this score the intended metre is more clearly defined with vertical bar lines.

There is a useful development between the two scores. The first is open to interpretation and there is no partner with whom to keep in time. In the second the metre is strongly implied. This is worth testing out with children in school when it fits into the unit of work in progress. Graphic scores are always open to a degree of interpretation so there is room for some creativity.

Developing rhythmic awareness

We have already introduced you to another useful strategy for developing rhythmic work and that is the pulse grid. You have already seen this used to aid composing processes. It is a most useful 'scaffold' for a teacher to use to interact with the children and for them then to develop their own work independently. A single line can be developed into a set of four lines.

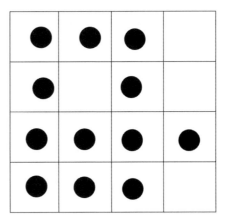

The children get used to reading the dots as claps or any other body sound that is chosen. Then they can progress to using pictures to aid the important shift from including single beats in each pulse square to two half-beats. In the last chapter we introduced the idea of using the two characters Rosie and Jim. The appeal of using characters that can be demonstrated as dolls will work well with younger children. Hence the score:

Can be read as   ⊓ | ⊓ |

At the next stage the mnemonics that we introduced earlier, 'coffee' and 'tea' for ⊓ and | , will be useful for children. When talking to the children you can describe a rhythm as being, for instance, *coffee coffee tea tea* and will be understood. Then the children themselves will start to use the language when working with each other.

It is understood that such a system limits the range of rhythms that can be used, but in other contexts, when not notating, more complex patterns can be introduced. However, throughout Key Stage 2 the Kodály rhythm system can be expanded in order to notate more complex rhythms if this feature of music is to be developed. The pulse grid can be used with *coffees* and *teas* as a structure for creating longer rhythm patterns

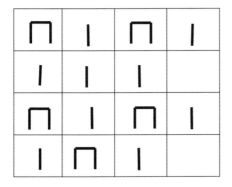

In parallel with this, other ways of building rhythmic skill and understanding can be developed, particularly through language. As the words coffee and tea were useful in defining simple rhythm patterns, longer phrases can be used to create longer rhythms.

PRACTICAL TASK PRACTICAL TASK PRACTICAL TASK PRACTICAL TASK PRACTICAL TASK

Learning objective: To understand how children establish the connection between words and rhythm.

The children can learn a simple rhyme such as:

Jelly on the plate
Jelly on the plate
Wibble wobble wibble wobble
Jelly on the plate

Then establish the habit of making sure children say the rhyme, clap the pattern while saying it and finally clap the rhythm alone, summarised in the following:

Say it – say it and play it – play it

Then see if the children can tell you what the rhythm of each line will be in coffees and teas.

You can take a different approach by using cards with defined rhythms on them so that children can be creative in their approach.

Teaching example

The short phrases met earlier in the practical task of the 'Later years' section can be written on cards as follows in appropriate colours. There should be multiple sets of each card.

Brown wavy line | ⊓ | z

Purple triangle | | ⊓ |

Blue circle | z | |

Green line | z | z

In order to introduce the cards the teacher helps the children to say the rhythm words to a steady pulse and in a strictly metrical way. She holds up a card, says the name and the class repeat it. Then the teacher has a set of, say, two cards of each in a shuffled pack. The children have one each. The teacher holds up the card at the top of the pack and counts four. Any children with that card chant the words on the card to a count of four. This way they get to know the rhythm words really well.

There is a range of possibilities from here on. The teacher might place two cards on the board for a small group to repeat as an ostinato. Meanwhile others can chant a set of four rhythm words one after the other. These rhythms can then be replaced by body sounds. An interesting way of performing these could be to split the larger group into four so that each plays the rhythm of the words on one card with a different body sound and then this forms into a cycle that runs three or four times. The ostinato makes a background accompaniment to these sounds.

The limitation of this approach is that in order for the words to fit to the pulse they need to be spoken in rather a stilted way. Work can also be done in the later years of Key Stage 1 using rhymes and raps which although generally conforming to the pulse may have some freer patterns within each line. The example you will meet in the section about language and music in Chapter 7 has this irregularity.

The monkey and the lion
Got to talking one day.
Monkey looked down and said, 'Lion,
I hear you're king in every way.

It is quite possible to lock it into a regular pattern and to deliver it like a rap by, for instance, rushing 'Lion I hear', because the natural, but perhaps less interesting, pattern would leave these out.

Monkey looked down and said,
You're king in every way

PRACTICAL TASK PRACTICAL TASK PRACTICAL TASK PRACTICAL TASK PRACTICAL TASK

Learning objective: To become more confident in understanding the correspondence between rhyme and song.

Write out the rhyme met earlier, 'Jelly on the plate', with two spare lines between each line of words.

Say the rhyme to yourself and keep the pulse with one hand slapping a knee. Now mark in with a dot above the syllables that coincide with each beat. Each line fits to four beats. Watch for the empty beat at the end of lines one and two. These will need a Z above them to mark the rest. Now clap the first line and decide whether the beats should be *coffees* or *teas*.

This survey of some activities should give you a framework of progression that you can use to pin activities in other musical elements to. However, it as well to remember that the way in which something is taught in music is as important to its suitability for a particular group of children as the content.

A SUMMARY OF **KEY POINTS**

> **Early musical experiences such as parents singing or children making musical play are fundamental to children's musical development, particularly in the pre-school years.**

> **Children's musical experiences during the school years include informal music-making on the playground, often incorporating familiar pop songs.**

> **The natural range of children's voices at different ages needs to be the starting point for developing singing but not the end point.**

> **The link between movement and music is very significant in the Early Years, as evidenced by children's singing games and dances.**

> **Children's levels of physical control need to be taken into account when setting expectations of instrumental playing.**

> **Particular teaching strategies should meet the needs of children at specific ages, particularly the increasing responsiveness to the expressive qualities of music.**

> **Some musical elements require more systematic development. Duration is one of these. Simple forms of graphic notation, both free form and the Kodály system help in this process.**

What next?

This chapter has been about really observing and understanding children and how they change as they grow up. This may be something of a shift from the state of mind you were in when you started your programme. Initially trainees find that they focus on their own techniques and strategies. You may have found the same, but then when you have some security in managing a class and engaging the children in activities, the focus does begin to move to the children. See this chapter as an opportunity to reflect on what makes the children receptive to the music you do with them. What music do they make when left to their own devices and hence when are they ready for new ideas and challenges that you offer them? Then, to take this line of thinking on further, consider the kind of challenges that they take on in other subjects that may have a parallel in music education. One example would be the development of literacy in language learning that has an equivalent in musical notation.

To develop the work on rhythm using 'Jelly on the plate' further, follow Unit 10 from the QCA scheme for music.

REFERENCES REFERENCES **REFERENCES** REFERENCES **REFERENCES** REFERENCES

Anderman, E.M., Anderman, L.H. and Griesinger, T. (1999) The relation of present and possible academic selves during early adolescence to grade point average and achievement goals. *Elementary School Journal*, 100, 3–17

Beard, R.M. (1969) *An outline of Piaget's developmental psychology*. London: Routledge and Kegan Paul

Bjørkvold (1989) *The muse within: Creativity and communication, song and lay from childhood through maturity* (W.H. Halverson, trans.). New York: Harper Collins

Csikszentmihalyi, M. (1990) *Flow: The psychology of optimal experience*. New York: Harper and Row

DeCasper, A. and Fifer, W. (1980) Of human bonding: Newborns prefer their mothers' voices. *Science*, 208 (4448), 1174–76

DfES (2007) *Practice Guidance for the Early Years Foundation Stage*. Nottingham: DfES Publications

Driver, A. (1936) *Music and movement*. London: Oxford University Press

Dutoit, C-L (1965) *Music Movement Therapy*. Dalcroze Society

Grudgeon, E. (2001) 'We like singing the Spice Girl songs and we like Tig and Stuck in the Mud': Girl's traditional games on two playgrounds. In J.C. Bishop and M. Curtis (eds), *The state of play: Perspectives on children's oral traditions in the school playground* (pp 98–114). Milton Keynes: Open University Press

Keetman, G. (1974) *Elementaria* (trans. Murray, M.) London: Schott and Co. Ltd.

Lawton, D. (1973) *Social change, educational theory and curriculum planning*. London: Hodder and Stoughton

Littleton, D. (1991) *Influence of play settings on pre-school children's music and play behaviours*. Doctoral dissertation. The University of Texas at Austin, USA. Dissertation Abstracts International, 52(4), 1198. University Microfilms Order No. 91 – 28294).

Marsh, K. and Young, S. (2006) Musical play. In McPherson, G.E. (ed.) *The child as musician*, Oxford: Oxford University Press

McPherson, G.E. (ed.) (2006) *The child as musician*. Oxford: Oxford University Press

Marsh, H.W. (1990) A multidimensional hierarchical model of self-concept: Theoretical and empirical justification. *Educational Psychology Review*, 2, 77–172

Merrill-Mirsky, C. (1986) *Girl's clapping games in three Los Angeles schools*. Yearbook for Traditional Music, Vol.18, pp47–59

Moorhead, G. and Pond, D. (1978) Music of young children. (Reprinted from the 1941–1951 editions.) Santa Barbara, CA: Pillsbury Foundation for the Advancement of Music Education

O'Connel, D. (2003) *The effects of prenatal music experience on one-week-old infants' timbre discrimination of selected auditory stimuli*. (Doctor of Philosophy, University of North Carolina at Greensboro). Dissertations Abstracts International, 64/06-A,2018 (University Microfilms No.3093879).

Opie, I. and Opie, P. (1988) *The singing game*. Oxford: Oxford University Press

Pugh, A. and Pugh, L. (1998) *Music in the Early Years*. London: Routledge

Renwick, J.M. and MacPhearson, G.E. (2006) *Age related changes in the young musicians' beliefs about their autonomy, competence and values*.

Sundin, B. (1960/1998) Musical creativity in the first six years. In B. Sundin, G.E. McPherson and G. Folkstad (eds) *Children composing: Research in music education* 1998 (pp35–56). Lund, Sweden: Malmo Academy of Music, Lund University

Suzuki, S. (1969) (trans. Suzuki, W.) *Nurtured by love: A new approach to education.* Smithtown, New York: Exposition Press

Wigfield, A. et al. (1997) Changes in children's competence beliefs and subjective task values across the elementary school years: A 3-year study. *Journal of Educational Psychology*, 89, 451–69

Young (2003). Time space structuring in spontaneous play on educational percussion instruments among three- and four-year-olds. *British Journal of Music Education*, 20, 45–59

FURTHER READING FURTHER READING **FURTHER READING** FURTHER READING

Classroom song and musical activity books

Sanderson, A. (1995) *Banana splits – ways into part-singing*. London: A & C Black

Gadsby, D. and Harrop, B. (2002) *Flying around*. London: A & C Black

Baxter, K. (1978) *Pompaleeri Jig*. Exeter: E.J Arnold –Wheaton Pergamon Press

QCA (2000) A scheme of work for key stages 1 and 2 – Music. London: DfEE

Audio CD

Ben Badoo in *Introduction to World Music* – Womad 2003

7
Music across the curriculum

By the end of this chapter you will begin to understand and know about:

- how music may combine with and support other subjects in meaningful ways;
- a range of specific subject combinations with music;
- a wide range of cross-curricular activities including music.

This chapter addresses the following Professional Standards for QTS:
Q6, Q8, Q10, Q14, Q15, Q17, Q18, Q22, Q23, Q25a, Q25b, Q32

A general background to cross-curricular thinking

The government initiative Excellence and Enjoyment (2003) and more recently the New Primary Strategy (2007) have shifted emphasis from a discrete focus on literacy and numeracy to a recognition that it is through a rich contextual use in other subjects that standards are more effectively raised in the key skills. This is encapsulated in the statements that making the strategy work lies in:

> empowering primary schools to take control of their curriculum, and to be more innovative...
> encouraging schools to....embed the principles of effective teaching and learning both in literacy and numeracy and across the curriculum.. [and to] .. make the most of links between different areas and provide opportunities for children to have a wide range of learning experiences. (DfES, 2003)

Despite these encouraging signs there may also be an implicit warning. The history of cross-curricular work in primary schools is one of variable degrees of success. However, if the reasons for its weaknesses are understood there is no reason why the school system should not make a better job of the enterprise this time around. In the early 1990s in parallel with the advent of the National Curriculum, Alexander et al. criticised the practice in primary school of teaching through topics on the grounds that the work children were doing was lacking rigour and progressive acquisition of skills and understanding.

> Over the last few decades the progress of primary pupils has been hampered by the influence of highly questionable dogmas which have led to excessively complex classroom practices and devalued the place of subjects in the curriculum. The resistance to subjects at the primary stage is no longer tenable. (Alexander et al., 1992)

The links between subjects were often superficial or did not support key understandings in either subject. Music may have suffered from such weak links being made, as for instance, the song 'Five little frogs sitting on a log' does not support a topic on wildlife in ponds in any useful way. However, the process of subtraction in the song would support mathematics. The song will bring subtraction vividly to life and require children to actually exercise mathematical skill in a different context.

Three ways of making purposeful links between subjects were identified in the SCAA document *Planning the Curriculum at KS 1 and 2* (1994):

- one subject exercises skills learnt in the other;
- one subject adds conceptually to the other subject through common understandings and knowledge;
- one subject provides a useful stimulus for work in another.

In the light of present interest in different learning styles we should add the following:

- one subject may provide a different teaching or learning style to the other.

REFLECTIVE TASK

Learning objective: To consider the following teaching episode in terms of the above ways of linking subjects and through the analysis begin to understand how subject links work effectively.

The teacher reads the children the opening chapter of *The Iron Man* by Ted Hughes. He divides the first part into five sections, each about a paragraph long, but also each containing an episode of the story. The class is divided into five equivalent groups and each is given a photocopy of one of the episodes. They consider the mood or character of the passage and then select instruments that they feel will be suitable to express these. The teacher adds the instructions that particular sounds should accompany particular events, such as the red eyes of the Iron Man sweeping the countryside, and that each group should have one tuned percussion instrument on which to play an ostinato melody. The children then work independently on the project until the teacher brings them together. As he reads the story the groups play the relevant music and the teacher records the performance. The recording is played back to the children and they appraise what they hear. The teacher allows some time for making additions or changes to the music and then there is a re-recording and final evaluation.

Identify how the music activity enhances the experience of reading the text. Consider what the teacher learns about children's understanding of the text.

There is more than one way of organising these links. Sometimes the cross-curricular linking may be from one lesson to the next with a common theme between them; in other situations the lesson itself may include more than one subject; otherwise teachers may get together, pool their interests and expertise and plan for a combined class project.

Music links with subjects

Music as a methodology

Music may be considered a methodology in itself in the way that drama is. Like drama, it may take a little more organisation or it may require more energetic presentation but the result will often be a more engaged class and a more memorable experience. It is worth remembering that music in the primary school is largely a social activity and this makes it attractive to children. However, we need to resist the notion of only adding 'fun' to a subject through singing, which implies that we are sugaring the pill of a less attractive subject.

We can explore the ways that music can support another subject through looking at some examples in particular subjects.

Literacy and music

It is fully recognised, and this is by no means a new idea, that literacy is learned most effectively through its use in meaningful contexts. To make this happen the link between literacy and music can work both ways: music may support a lesson in which literacy is the prime focus, or the use of speaking and listening in particular may be enhanced in a music lesson.

In Chapter 1 we mentioned the importance of musical activities in developing phonic awareness, as described in the QCA document *Progression in Phonics* (2001) and throughout *Letters and Sounds: Phase 1* (2007). The documents advocate general listening activities to discriminate between qualities of sound as the basis of developing knowledge of, and skill in, fine differences in language. *Letters and Sounds* sets out a range of musical activities in Phase One (for Early Years settings).

1. General sound discrimination - environmental sounds: Taking children for a walk and collecting sounds as a means of encouraging good listening habits or making shakers out of opaque containers and filling them with mystery materials (rice, pebbles, coins, etc.).
2. General sound discrimination – instrumental sounds: After general familiarisation with instrument sounds, a set is laid out on the floor and a child chooses one from an identical set to play. The class identifies the instrument.
3. General sound discrimination – body percussion: One child leads in the role of the Pied Piper playing their chosen instrument and moving in a particular way. The class follows imitating the movement. Use the activity to extend vocabulary about movement, e.g. fast – rapid, slow – lazily or carefully.
4. Rhythm and rhyme: Skipping to rhymes such as 'Here we go round the mulberry bush' or rock to 'See saw Marjorie Daw' and link this with moving to the sound of a rhythmic beat on an instrument.
6. Voice sounds: Have a wide repertoire of songs on tape or audio CD that the children can choose to listen to.

Further to 3 above, the song 'Slap the Sillies out' (Chapter 4) requires children to *be attentive and to know when to add sounds or move and when to be silent* (QCA (2001)).

Awareness of rhyme (4 above) can also contribute to this ability to discriminate between sounds. A nursery rhyme such as 'Miss Polly had a Dolly' has rhymes within the lines and repetition of rhyming words.

> *Miss Polly had a dolly*
> *Who was sick, sick, sick.*
> *So she phoned for the doctor*
> *To be quick, quick, quick.*

The children are soon able to identify the different consonants in initial positions: '**P**olly' and '**d**olly', '**s**ick' and '**qu**ick'. This rhyme may be found in *This Little Puffin* in which may also be found 'Old MacDonald had a farm' and 'The wheels on the bus', both good for developing phonical awareness.

In Chapter 3 we wrote about the importance of exploring the voice (6 above). This might be in an activity such as 'Have you brought your quiet voice?' (Chapter 1). Additionally such a rhyme as 'Eensy Weensy Spider climbed up the wall' encourages children to play with language and to explore similar but significant differences in language, e.g. the initial letters in **E**ensy **W**eensy.

Having established the foundations, music activities can then continue through Key Stages 1 and 2 to provide diversity to teaching methods in literacy.

The speaking of poetry or chant is as much a musical as a literary activity. Consider the traditional American rhyme that follows which has some regularities such as word rhyme and regular scansion which are associated with song but also some delightfully irregular lines.

> The monkey and the lion
> Got to talking one day.
> Monkey looked down and said, 'Lion,
> I hear you're king in every way.
> But I know somebody
> Who do not think that is true –
> He told me he could whip
> The living daylights out of you.'
> Lion said, 'Who?'
> Monkey said, 'Lion,
> He talked about your mama
> And talked about your grandma, too,
> And I'm too polite to tell you
> What he said about you.'
> Lion said, 'Who said what? Who?'
> Monkey in the tree,
> Lion on the ground.
> Monkey kept on signifying
> But he didn't come down…

The chant can be performed using musical features that we have become familiar with. The musical elements of dynamics, timbre, pitch and tempo in particular will bring life to the performance (note Chapter 1). Monkey can have a high voice and Lion a low one (pitch), they may also have particular tone qualities (timbre) and Monkey could speak fast while Lion speaks slowly (tempo). The last line can be slowed down to give emphasis to the words 'didn't come down'.

PRACTICAL TASK PRACTICAL TASK PRACTICAL TASK PRACTICAL TASK PRACTICAL TASK

Find your own rhyme with a strong rhythm to it. Practice reciting it with a variety of dynamics, timbre, pitch and tempo.

It is also worth noting that the driving forward of the rhythm in such rhymes is very helpful for children with speaking difficulties because they are carried along by the pace and predictability of the rhythm. Also the structure of poetry can be made clear to children when spoken in a particular way or sung to a familiar tune. This also makes the words more memorable. Children will memorise the words of songs with ease and the memorising of language forms will add to the quality of their own general language use. The simple act of reading words in patterns and with repetitions will become useful reading exercises in themselves.

Similar to the opportunities for reading while engaged in music activity, there are wider opportunities for specific language development. These are pointed out in the QCA *Scheme for Music: Teacher's handbook*:

> spoken language also plays a significant part in enabling children to develop their musical understanding, and music can make a significant contribution to the development of literacy. Children can develop language skills by:
> - singing songs with attention to meaning and diction and an awareness of phrase;
> - using their voices creatively and descriptively when composing and performing;
> - discussing musical features and describing sounds and how they are used in their own and other people's music;
> - negotiating with others in group and class music-making activities;
> - collecting information using reference books, CD-ROMs, e-mail and the internet;
> - asking questions to help them clarify tasks, discover other views and increase their understanding;
> - responding to questions that require:
>   - analysis and factual recall, for example 'What did you do?' 'What sounds were used?'
>   - reasoning, for example 'Why did you do that?'
>   - evaluation, for example 'What went well?' 'What could have been better?' 'What effect does it create?'
>   - creativity, for example 'How will you make it better?' 'Could that be done in a different way?' 'What else have you done that might help you decide what to do next?' (2000, p21)

In the Literacy Strategy documents music is seen very largely as being in the service of literacy. However, despite this, the musical experiences are substantial in themselves. This balance is one that needs to be monitored carefully.

Links with history

Recorded music to listen to could be used as background to activities associated with an historical topic. The familiarity with the music can be useful when children come to listen more critically. It may be especially useful to use the music in association with drama or dance. The children can respond to the period features of the music such as the gracefulness of Tudor dance or the romantic sentiment of Victorian song.

Teaching example

Listening to recorded music, 'Courante' from *Terpsichore* by Michael Praetorius (1610)

The teacher plays a range of instruments, some of which sound like those heard in the recorded music. She then lays them out on the floor for all the children to see. The children are directed to point to or write down the name of the instruments that look like the ones they think they are hearing. For example:

a recorder;
a glockenspiel;
a single-sided drum (tambour);
a tambourine.

Now try learning this simple Tudor dance and discover the degree to which the character of the music can be felt through the movement.

PRACTICAL TASK PRACTICAL TASK PRACTICAL TASK PRACTICAL TASK PRACTICAL TASK

Learning objectives:

- To understand the range of purposeful links music can make with other areas of the curriculum.
- To understand the importance of making curriculum links that enhance understanding or skill between subjects.
- To know a simple Tudor dance (pavan) so that it can be carried out as a classroom activity.

Use any pavan music (see Appendix, *Let's Make Tudor Music*) to learn the dance to. Any slow period piece with a count (metre) of 4 will do.

This dance is very basic and is made up of two steps, simples and doubles.
Simple left: left foot steps to the left and the right foot closes with it
Simple right: right foot steps to the right and the left foot closes with it
Double forward: leading with the right walk three steps forward and close with the left foot
Double back: Do the reverse closing with the left foot.

Now put it all together:

- simple left and simple right;
- double forward;
- simple right and simple left;
- double back.

REFLECTIVE TASK
REFLECTIVE TASK

Learning objective: To clarify in your own mind how movement and music are linked.

As you did in the activity above, so children may learn about music by responding through movement. Consider the advantages of this approach and what in particular the children are learning by experiencing music in this way.

This is a richly cross-curricular activity in that not only are there links with the history curriculum but also PE. The sound of the music itself will be distinctly Tudor (or Renaissance, as referred to in Chapter 2) partly through the sound of the instruments, e.g. recorder and lute, but also because the dance is slow and stately. Children can compare this with the modern dance music they enjoy. The difference will give a strong sense of the *characteristic features of the periods and societies studied* (History National Curriculum Key Stage 2, 2a). The slow and formal tempo of the pavan contrasts greatly with the fast and relaxed modern dance music. Could a performance of the dance be a way to *communicate their knowledge and understanding of history in a variety of ways* (5c)? The performance could be to the class next door or could be part of a presentation at a Friday assembly.

Now think about how a song could link with the history curriculum. The following is a ballad which was sung by a ballad seller to a contemporary dance tune. He would sell copies of the words to the crowds that he attracted (but I imagine his market was rather limited when we consider the literacy level of the times). The ballad tells the story of the

Armada in chauvinistic fashion with no concessions to a view of history that might be told by the vanquished. A note in the margin of the National Curriculum about historical interpretation says that *interpretations reflect the circumstances in which they are made, the available evidence, and the intentions of those who make them*. We can be very clear about the intentions of this ballad singer.

King Phi - lip call'd his Ad -mi - ral And told him not to stay - a.
But to des -troy both man and boy And so to come a - way - a.

And so to come a - way - a And so to come a - way - a

2 Their navy was well victualled
With biscuit, pease and bacon,
They'd many a gun to make us run
But I think they were mistaken.
But I think they were mistaken.

3 They coasted round about our land,
And so came in by Dover,
But we had men set on them then,
And threw the rascals over.
And threw the rascals over.

4 The Queen was then at Tilbury,
What more could we desire - a?
Sir Francis Drake for her sweet sake
Did set them all on fire - a
Did set them all on fire - a

REFLECTIVE TASK

If the class has learnt the song 'The Armada', discussed the words and performed it, what do you consider the song contributes to their historical understanding? Use the history National Curriculum programmes of study that follow as a frame of reference (historical interpretation has already been discussed above):

- chronological understanding;
- historical enquiry.

Links with the other arts

Links between the arts are a special case. Each art form can act as a stimulus for work in the other. The common thread between them is usually the idea that is being expressed. In one activity it may be the expression of mood; in another the structure of the piece of work. It is important to be clear about this common strand because it is the main objective of the lesson. As the lesson progresses you need to refer to it so that the children grow in understanding of the idea itself and how it is used.

Poetry

> ### CLASSROOM STORY
>
> Emma, a postgraduate trainee, was focusing on 'performance poetry' in literacy. In a previous lesson she had read 'Macavity: The Mystery Cat' by TS Eliot. The children had talked about how Macavity is described in the poem and what they thought about him as a character.
>
> In this next lesson she played Andrew Lloyd Webber's version of 'Macavity: The Mystery Cat' from the Musical *Cats* to provide the children with an example of how poems can be performed in different ways. The children thoroughly enjoyed listening to the music and asked for it to be played at different times in the days following the lesson. They were very engaged when listening to the words of the poem and how they were performed to demonstrate the different personalities of Macavity. Listening to the music led well into a variety of different group activities. For example, one group discussed the positive and negative descriptions of Macavity while another group imagined what kinds of adventures they would have if they were Macavity.
>
> Emma found that listening to a different kind of performance of the poem stimulated the children's learning and helped them to grasp the mood as well as providing a musical stimulus for their own poetry writing later in the week.

In this classroom story Emma uses the music to bring life to the character of the cat in the poem. We can imagine how the English lesson might progress into children's writing about character. In the following activity it is the shape and structure of the music that help children create abstract visual forms.

At the heart of the activity, then, is the idea of form (or structure) and shape in both music and art. When assessing the children's responses, the teacher will consider the level at which the children are understanding the way in which the melody is made up of musical phrases.

> ### CLASSROOM STORY
> **A Year 5 class**
>
> Jane chose to combine music with an art lesson for her Year 5 class. She worked with the class in the hall. Lining paper was rolled out on the floor and she positioned the children spaced out along both sides. They had large varied coloured chalks to work with. To prepare the children she directed them to stand in a wide circle around the working area. They were to pretend they had large paintbrushes in their hands and to paint large shapes in the air following the up and down contour of the melody. Next, she put recorded music on for the children to listen to, 'Walking in the Air' from the film *The Snowman*. Some children could clearly hear the ups and downs in the tune but others just followed the mood of the piece. This did not concern the teacher because she expected to have different outcomes. When they had completed these large movements following the tune twice through, she directed the children to position themselves by the paper and when the music was repeated the children were to follow the same up and down movements that they had created with their imaginary paint brushes, but this time with fine motor movements, creating long sweeping shapes on the paper. Sometimes they had to negotiate their way past other children but in the end, after a few times through, they produced a rich texture of different lines that enclosed interesting spaces which were painted in at a later point.

The children were completely absorbed in the activity and so were enabled to listen with concentration to the music for an extended period of time.

Rebecca teaches Year 1

After a visit to an aquarium the children created an 'Under the Sea' collage as a whole class. Children then worked in groups which each had a different feature from the collage to represent through sound, e.g. bubbles in the water, a shark or small fish. From a set of instruments available to them they explored which they could use. One child at a time took turns to be the conductor and pointed to various parts of the collage, at which the relevant group played the music they had devised.

As discussed in Chapter 2, listening to recorded music can suggest more than character in a story. It can stimulate ideas about what the characters are doing, where they are doing it and some elements of narrative. The orchestral music 'The Tuilerie Gardens' from *Pictures at an Exhibition* by Mussorgsky could very easily be painting a musical picture of a children's playground. Each musical idea might be a group of children playing a game. The children can imagine the games being played and describe them in words. The games interrupt each other as so often happens in real life, and this introduces conflict to the story.

Dance

Music is clearly a very important part of dance. However, I wonder how often the musical aspects are considered as part of the music curriculum. We have mentioned this in Chapter 2 on listening to recorded music because it is such an effective way for children to respond to music. In this chapter when discussing links with history I mentioned teaching the historical dance, the pavan, which in its dignified manner makes both a point about the place of dance in its own time and gives opportunities for controlled and elegant movement. There follow some examples of how a Year 1 teacher used work with instruments in her PE lessons.

CLASSROOM STORY
Rebecca teaches Year 1

Dance lesson

Children listened to recordings of the sounds of fireworks and developed actions and movements to represent the different types, e.g. Catherine wheel, rocket, sparkler, bangers. Then they chose instruments and decided how they could play the instrument to represent different types of fireworks, e.g. shaking a maraca to represent a sparkler, a tambour to represent a banger, or shaking a tambourine slowly getting faster to represent a Catherine wheel.

One group of children were chosen to play their firework sounds in a sequence, then the other children listened and moved according to which firework they thought was being represented.

PE warm-up activity with a focus on pitch

Rebecca had two chime bars – one high note and one low. She played the notes before the children started the activity so that they could hear and identify each note whether high or low. The children then travelled round the hall; when they heard the high note they stretched up high, when they heard the low note they tucked up low to the floor.

Sometimes she used a tambour or tambourine which she played fast or slow. Then the children listened to the tempo of the beat and moved accordingly.

Music and modern foreign languages

Entitlement to modern foreign languages is being introduced into primary schools in 2010. There are two principal ways in which music can contribute:

- memorising vocabulary;
- learning standard phrases.

Some standard vocabulary can be learnt very easily in song form. In the following example children can learn the months of the year in German.

Die Jahresuhr

Here Claire, a Year 4 BA primary education trainee, teaches colours in Spanish.

CLASSROOM STORY

During her third and fourth year teaching placements in a primary school Claire taught Spanish to both Year 5 and Year 6 pupils that had no previous experience in the subject.

She used the tune of 'London Bridge is falling down' to teach Spanish colours with the aid of flashcards to add the visualisation of each colour as it was sung. She chose several children to stand in a line at the front of the class in the correct order of the song and to hold up their colour as it was sung.

One verse of the song is as follows:

Blanco rojo verde azul,   White red green blue,
Verde azul, verde azul.   Green blue, green blue.
Blanco rojo verde azul   White red green blue
Amarillo   Yellow
(*Note*: The final 'e' of 'verde' is elided with the 'a' of 'azul'.)

The repetition of vocabulary is also helpful in a song, so long as the children pronounce carefully each time, as in the following French versions of familiar English songs.

'If you're happy and you know it'. (If you like mathematics clap your hands)

Si tu aimes les maths, frappe les mains,
Si tu aimes les maths, frappe les mains,
Si tu aimes les maths, Si tu aimes les maths,
Si tu aimes les maths, frappe les mains.

'Heads shoulders knees and toes' has movements that help with the meaning.

La tête, les épaules, les genoux et les pieds,
La tête, les épaules, les genoux et les pieds,
Les yeux, les oreilles, la bouche et le nez,
La tête, les épaules, les genoux et les pieds.

Learning standard phrases is more integrated into the language lesson as would be the following in German 'Suzanne, what do you want? I want an apple. Liam what do you want? I want a cherry' sung to the notes g and e.

The children will remember the tune with the phrase and the combination makes the phrase all the more memorable. Note the use of the calling notes g and e, last met in Chapter 3.

CLASSROOM STORY

Claire decided to teach Spanish through song as she felt it would be easier for the children to retain the new vocabulary. She used familiar nursery rhymes to sing to as the children would be able to recognise and remember these more easily. She also added actions to aid in the understanding of the songs' meaning. The songs often showed both sides of a dialogue so the children were also able to learn conversation and communication skills alongside the new vocabulary.

One of the songs was used to teach 'how are you' and how to give a reply in Spanish.

¿Como esta? ¿Como esta? ¿Como esta? ¿Que tal _(name)_?

The children would be sitting in a circle and pass a Spanish object, such as a fan or castanets, around the circle while singing. Then they would give the name of the child holding the fan after the question '¿Que tal?' and that child would have to reply in Spanish to say how they were feeling with a phrase such as, 'Muy bien gracias'.

Music linked to ICT

The combination with ICT is yet another kind of link in which it acts as a medium or methodology. At secondary level music technology has become a very considerable part of the music curriculum. Performing with electronic instruments, composing on computer and making use of amplification and recording facilities have become standard components of music lessons. At primary level these formats are present but at a less significant level.

Using electronic keyboards is beginning to be a particularly useful addition to the range of sounds achievable in the classroom. Many children will be learning to play keyboards and they may have the facility to use button chords in the left hand to accompany melodies in the right. This adds the dimension of harmony to the work in the classroom if children's extra-curricular learning can be incorporated.

Examples of the use of keyboards:

- The keyboard rhythm function combined with the auto chord accompaniment is used by a teacher as a background to a rhythm game. She fits her counts of four beats to the pulse of the rhythm as she claps rhythmic phrases. The children echo her and fit their rhythm to the pulse on the keyboard. Not only are the children learning about rhythm patterns but they are also refining their skill in keeping in time. The teacher then resets the tempo control down to do the same exercise slightly slower.
- Children use a special tone called 'landscape' to create a dream-like atmosphere. They only play three notes, but this is the background to a composition using percussion instruments.

As seen in Chapter 5 computer software has a very important role in the widening range of creative possibilities especially as children become more competent in the use of such technical tools. Software that enables children to write compositions using Western notation have become very sophisticated. The most widely used of these is 'Sibelius', which has a junior version. For those children who are already music readers through instrumental tuition this can be a very useful tool to record their musical ideas. However, generally speaking other means such as graphic scores and audio recording are more useful.

Audio recording

Recording facilities for children are in transitional developmental stage. In the recent past the use of small cassette recorders was common and children can and still make good use of these despite the poor quality. A couple of points to note are:

- making sure that the recording starts after counting five seconds to avoid recording while the lead-in tape is running;
- keeping very resonant and loud percussion instruments like cymbals and the shekere further away from the microphone.

Using a mobile phone recorder can often be quite satisfactory for a small group to hear, but if the class is to hear the result a lead is needed to connect to an amplifier. Increasingly small digital recorders are in use and can be connected to a computer for playback.

Mathematics

It is interesting to reflect that those who like mathematics or use it as part of their work also have a liking for music and it is commonly said that music and mathematics are the most abstract forms in their own fields. An anonymous commentator has this to say:

Mathematics is music for the mind; music is mathematics for the soul.

Yet despite this affinity, the ways in which the subjects interact seem either to be at a very fundamental level in which numeric relationships are not present, or at a complex level which is unsuited to children of primary age. I have tried to interest a child in measuring the relative lengths of the brass tubing created by the different valve combinations for the notes of a scale on a cornet but I feel sure the interest lay more with the teacher than the child despite his being a cornet player.

However, at a simple level, number songs can make a useful contribution to the mental mathematics period in a mathematics lesson. Often it is not the common element of numeric relationships that makes this work but simply the usefulness of song in giving pace and enjoyment to some basic mathematical operations.

Sometimes the song may be about subtraction, as above; at other times it may be about working in multiples.

> Ten fat sausages sitting in a pan; *(show ten fingers, or line up ten children)*
> One went, 'pop!' and another went 'BANG!' *(clap hands or one child says 'pop' and the other 'bang!')*
> Eight fat sausages etc.

There follows an example of how a teacher uses music to help children appreciate number as a concept in time as well as space.

CLASSROOM STORY

Nicola taught her Year 2 class about sequencing.

She ensured that the children's concept of number is aural as well as visual by playing numbers of beats on a triangle. The children listen carefully for the next in a sequence, e.g. in steps of 2, 5, 10, etc.

Rebecca with her Year 1 class did something similar but linked this to the concept of pattern.

As well as sequencing beads on a string or pictures on a page she played three different instruments in a sequence. The children remembered the order and were able to repeat the sequence. This was differentiated by changing the number of instruments used or making the sequence more or less complex.

At a more complex level when developing rhythm patterns in compositions, some interest and deeper understanding of rhythm patterns can be achieved through looking at varied metres and how these can be broken down to create off-beat rhythms.

PRACTICAL TASK PRACTICAL TASK PRACTICAL TASK PRACTICAL TASK PRACTICAL TASK

Take the names from the tradition rhyme 'Solomon Grundy' and break these down into syllables:

⊓⊓   ⊓
Solomon   Grundy

Find as many different ways of combining these into a cycle, or bar, of between seven and twelve beats. For example: Solomon Solomon Grundy 'eight beats'

By clapping on the first of each set of two or three beats you create interesting off-beat patterns with a Latin American flavour.

This is the musical equivalent of asking children how many addition sums making between 7 and 12 they can create just using 2s and 3s. The interesting difference is that the order in music is all important but in addition it is not.

If you have the patience it is then rather fun to 'find' the multiple of, say, seven and nine by the following method:

Have two players playing patterns of seven and nine in any pattern they like, e.g.:

Player one: ⊓ ⊓ ⊓⊓

Player two: ⊓ ⊓⊓⊓⊓

If the pattern is played by tapping on a table, the first in each set should be on something that sounds different, like a set of keys for one and a CD case for the other, e.g.

Player one: **Keys** left right left right left left

Player two: **Case** left right left right left right left left

When both the keys and the CD case sounds coincide, the multiple (number of beats) has been reached. It certainly is not as quick as using memorised tables but good fun can be had and it does sound intriguing.

Links with science

There is a natural link with the science topics of 'sound' and 'materials' as exemplified in this classroom story from a postgraduate trainee.

CLASSROOM STORY

Emma was in her final placement with a Year 5 class. As part of their science topic on 'Changing sounds' they were exploring how pitch could be altered. Their learning objective was to *understand that pitch and loudness are different and can be altered*. She began by playing three drums of different sizes and asked the children to note down which they thought had the lowest or highest pitch. She developed this by playing each drum loudly and quietly to emphasise that the pitch remains the same. The children then watched a video clip of timpani (large orchestral drums) being played in Britten's *Young People's Guide to the Orchestra* while thinking about how the drum skin can be altered to change the pitch of the drum.

They then moved on to think about stringed instruments and Emma demonstrated how pitch can be altered on a stringed instrument. She showed the children her violin, then demonstrated the different ways of playing the instrument and the different sounds that are created through bowing, plucking and so on. She played each string and then demonstrated

> how the pitch of the string could be altered by adjusting the pegs and what happens to the string when we do this.
>
> Using live instruments, showing instruments being played and involving the children in the lesson was extremely effective in demonstrating pitch and all the children developed a firm understanding of how pitch can be altered on different instruments.

The fact that vibrations create sound is the key idea in the sound section of the science curriculum. A lesson in which children become aware of the relationship can have musical outcomes as well as scientific. The children need to find the tangible and visible evidence of vibrations. They might strike a cymbal and then touch it. They might feel the vibrations in the string handle of a triangle. They might see vibrations in a low guitar string or drop rice onto a drum, strike it and watch the rice jump. They can test materials to see which ones vibrate and which don't.

It is also worth thinking about how children making their own instruments from scrap materials, as discussed in Chapter 3, may contribute to understanding the properties of materials. Also there is a contribution to be made to design and technology through this kind of activity.

Music across the curriculum in Early Years

CLASSROOM STORY

Suzanne uses music throughout the curriculum. This is one example of how music enhances the Early Years curriculum in her Reception class.

Personal, social and emotional development – group awareness
Circle time – Suzanne sends sounds around the circle, i.e. she makes a sound such as clap, clap, tap, tap and each child, one at a time, copies the sound as it goes around the circle.

Communication, language and literacy
- Suzanne calls this activity 'phonics aerobics' – she puts on a recorded piece of music. The children march in time to the music, show a letter card, then they say the corresponding phoneme and do the relevant 'Jolly Phonics' actions while marching to the music.
- Nursery rhymes – Suzanne claps or taps the rhythm of the nursery rhyme as they sing it.
- The children add instrument sounds to a story, e.g. 'Peace at last'. Then they decide what instrument would best depict each sound in the story.

Problem-solving, reasoning and number – making patterns
Suzanne models making a sound pattern, e.g. body sounds – tap, tap, tap, tap, clap, clap, tap, tap, tap, tap, clap, clap, etc. She uses a variety of instruments, e.g. two drum beats, one bell shake, two drum beats, one bell shake, etc.

Knowledge and understanding of the world
- Exploration and investigation using the senses
  - Finding the different sounds that can be made on a variety of instruments.
  - Go on a listening walk and find what sounds can be heard in the classroom or playground.
- Sense of chronology – learning traditional rhymes and songs that parents and grandparents learnt when they were at school.
- Cultures and beliefs – learning songs and rhymes from other cultures and adding percussion.

- Using the outdoor area – children have free access to instruments to play and create their own music individually or with friends.

Creative development
- Hearing sounds ('musical snap') – Suzanne organises two lines of five children back to back. The five children in each line have five different instruments, e.g. a triangle, drum, bell, tambourine and a wood block. A child in line A plays their instrument, the children in line B listen and the one with the same instrument plays a reply.
- In groups, children create their own music with instruments and then develop their own way of recording their music pictorially.
- Dance – the children listen to a piece of music and talk about how it makes them feel. They move accordingly, e.g. fast/slow/happy/sad music.

Physical development
- When children are moving they stop on the signal of a tambourine.
- Children make a small shape with their bodies, then Suzanne plays a musical instrument, e.g. shake of bells and the children stretch out to make a big shape.

Breadth of the curriculum – cultural diversity

In the National Curriculum for music the final section is labelled 'Breadth of study' and in this section can be found a reminder that the materials used (or repertoire) in music lessons should reflect diversity both historically and culturally. This will mean that the recorded music and the songs selected as well as the range of instruments should represent this range and diversity. The historic dimension has been reflected above in some depth and also in Chapter 2. You will note that cultural range is reflected in the examples given throughout the book. However, it is worth reflecting on diversity in music in a little more depth here. The principles underpinning this are not simply that the children themselves in the classes you teach will be drawn from diverse backgrounds but that all children growing up in a multicultural society are entitled to a curriculum that reflects the diversity of the country. Further than that, children are increasingly required to grasp the global dimension to issues and some appreciation of cultural variety will enable this wider understanding.

It is interesting to reflect on how this issue has altered since the 1970s and 1980s when folk music from around the world was commonly used in music programmes for schools. At that time the significance of the diversity was partly lost by the translation of the song lyrics into English. Clearly this was done with a good intention: that the children should understand the words. But the cultural integrity of the song was lost. In more recent years songs with original texts have become much more widely used to retain this important cultural element. But the choice of songs is made with care so that there is plenty of repetition or that the song itself will stand up to being repeated in a number of different ways. Hence variety comes through the performance rather than through the words.

The song 'Chu ah ai', a rice-pounding song from China, has also the advantage of being based on only three notes which incidentally are the same ones that 'It's raining it's pouring' is sung to. But also it is short and the words are repeated. The percussion, comprising gong, drum and wood block, is distinctively Chinese. The distinctive sound of percussion in Chinese music can be appreciated in performance. The song can be followed up by listening to Chinese music on recordings.

The small notes on the recorder part will add an interesting harmony

●.●● Read these as 'tick tock' on a two tone wood block. As you will see there are 4 beats in a bar and hence you play 8 half beats on the wood block.

/◌\ Play a gong or large cymbal with a large drum here. It does not need to be loud!

In a similar spirit the following children's song from Ghana needs no translation but is carried along by the actions.

The game:

Formation: Children seated in a circle with two stones (sticks, blocks) lying in front of them.

Action: At *up* the stones are picked up (one in each hand). At *down* the stones are placed on the floor in front of the neighbour on the right. These actions are repeated for each repetition of the phrase *obwisana*.

Variations: Only one stone is passed

Both stones are passed to the left

Using a pattern of 3 instead of 4 by picking up the stones on   ①
  clicking together on   ②
  passing to the left on   ③

As suggested in Chapter 2, one way of engaging children in listening is to encourage them to join in. The Cuban song 'Oye como va' by Carlos Santana lends itself to this approach and by adding a variety of percussion lines the children can pick up on the spirit of the samba music. However, these rhythms will work to any lively dance music to a metre of four.

TEACHING EXAMPLES

Carlos Santana meets Chocolate Heaven

Rhythms can be created from the following words and phrases.

A Say the words in rhythm

	1	2	3	4	1	2	3	4
1	a Mars		a Boost		a Flake		a Twix	
2	Mm	choc'late	Mm	choc'late	Mm	choc'late	Mm	choc'late
3	Gimme	choc'late	Gimme	choc'late	Gimme	choc'late	Gimme	choc'late
4	I want	choc'late	I want	choc'late	I want	choc'late	I want	choc'late
5	I	love	choc'	late	I	I	love it	—
6	I	love	choc'	late	I	I	I	love it

B Now say and play them body percussion	C Say and play instruments
1 Thigh slaps R L R L	Conga, drums
2 Stroke down inside of arm then clap clap	Guiros
3 Both hands reaching out, and pulling back	Shakers/maracas/rhythm eggs
4 Slap thighs R L R L	Bongos
5 Clap	Wood blocks/tulips/two tones
6 Clap	Cowbells/rattles

Start by just saying the words to a pulse. Then add the body percussion which matches the movement needed to play the instrument. This prepares the body and brain kinaesthetically actually playing the rhythms on instruments.

The following young teacher wanted to introduce children to music that was quite new. The challenge was to enjoy the unfamiliar but also to relate to what was recognisable.

CLASSROOM STORY

Asha was a BA QTS trainee in her final placement. Her Key Stage 1 class was responding to a recording of Indian classical music.

When listening to the music initially the children were quite bemused by the unfamiliar sounds and Hindi lyrics. Some giggled, while others tapped on their knees to the beats of the drum. However, the children particularly noticed and responded to the powerful sounds of the dhol drum as opposed to the subtler sounds of the sitar. They responded more when the drum played louder by playing their own instruments harder and faster. They did the same in the movement lesson by moving more strongly and faster to the louder and faster drum rhythm.

When familiar with the music the children began to appreciate it for its intrinsic qualities. However, it is worth noting that recordings of songs in foreign languages and more particularly in unfamiliar singing styles will nearly always provoke an embarrassed response to begin with.

A SUMMARY OF **KEY POINTS**

> **Cross-curricular thinking came into prominence in the 1960s. In the 1990s it came under criticism and only recently has been promoted again in the New National Strategy.**

> **Musical activity may be a strategy through which to teach other subjects.**

> **Literacy is the subject most commonly and most effectively linked with music. This is particularly apparent in the recent documents promoting a more exclusively phonically based approach to reading.**

> **Music links very effectively with history through most of the key understandings and skills such as chronological understanding, interpreting and use of sources and presentation of outcomes.**

> **Music and the other arts act mutually as stimuli for each other.**

> **Music is beginning to, and will more in the future, be a very useful means for consolidating vocabulary and short phrases in modern foreign languages.**

> **ICT provides a range of technologies that extend the range of what is possible in the composition and performance of music.**

> **Despite having much in common, music and mathematics are less comfortable as cross-curricular partners but there are some interesting possibilities.**

> **There are natural places for music to link with science in the topics 'Sounds and Materials'.**

> **Music can naturally fit into the whole Early Years curriculum.**

> **Being a powerful carrier of cultural values, music has much to contribute to children's knowledge and understanding of a range of cultures.**

What next?

Core standard 15 says that at the end of the qualifying year teachers should *have a secure knowledge and understanding of the subjects/curriculum areas they teach including: the contribution that their subjects/curriculum areas can make to cross-curricular learning, recent relevant developments, and related pedagogy.*

In the light of the waxing and waning of views regarding cross-curricular planning, it would not be surprising if schools were to be cautious in their implementation of the government's latest enthusiasm. However, this time, generally speaking, it is schools that are leading the way. Try to form a practical as well as an adventurous view about what music may contribute to learning across the curriculum. Above all, do not lose sight of the need to give children a balanced and progressive (as well as enjoyable) experience in music through their life in the primary school.

REFERENCES REFERENCES **REFERENCES** REFERENCES **REFERENCES** REFERENCES

Alexander, R., Rose, J. and Woodhead, C. (1992) *Curriculum organisation and classroom practice in primary schools, a Discussion Paper*. London: DES

DfEE and QCA (1999) *The National Curriculum – Handbook for teachers in England KS1 & 2*. London: DfEE Publications

DfES (2007) *Letter and sounds: principles and practice of high quality phonics: Primary National Strategy*.

QCA (2000) *Scheme for Music*. London: DfES Publications

QCA (2001) *The National Literacy Strategy – Progression in Phonics*. London: DfES Publications

QCA (2003) *Excellence and enjoyment – The Primary National Strategy*. London: DfES Publications

SCAA (1994) *Planning the curriculum at KS1 & 2*. London: DfES Publications.

Classroom song and story books

Boyd, B. et al. (1984) *Count me in*. London, Aylesbury: A & C Black

Hughes, T. (1968) *The iron man*. London & Boston: Faber and Faber

Matterson, E. (1969) *This Little Puffin*. Aylesbury: Puffin Books

Software

Junior Sibelius www.sibelius.com/products/

8
Organisation, planning, assessment and extra-curricular music

By the end of this chapter you should:

- understand that leading a performance means giving the class a note to sing on, how fast to go and when to start so that all children start together;
- understand that there are many opportunities for children to lead in music-making;
- understand that activities using instruments should include opportunities for the whole class and groups and can include: call and response, echoing, taking turns and circle games;
- understand that careful organisation for classroom instrumental activities is critical;
- give thought to the integration of children with special needs in music lessons;
- understand the part that extra-curricular music activities contribute to children's musical development and to the school community;
- have considered how children's musical skills gained in extra-curricular activities can be integrated in to classroom music-making.

This chapter addresses the following Professional Standards for QTS:
Q1, Q3b, Q10, Q11, Q12, Q14, Q15, Q17, Q18, Q19, Q22, Q23, Q25a, Q25b, Q25d, Q26a, Q30, Q31, Q32

Leading musical activities

The key factor in teaching music is whether you have enough skill and knowledge to be able to lead activities with confidence. Certainly there will be activities that all can lead with confidence. They may not require a strong and well-pitched singing voice or require much experience of participation in musical activities. Many of the creative activities mentioned throughout the book do not require a teacher to lead with a beat or to establish a starting note for a song. They require a teacher who can lead with enthusiasm and is adventurous in approach.

There are specific approaches particular to singing mentioned in Chapter 3 but whenever you are leading, starting and finishing are key aspects. Starting a song yourself requires a lead in two musical elements: tempo and pitch. The reason groups or conductors count in is simply to ensure that everyone can feel the beat. It really will not matter what you count; usually it is 'one, two, three, four', but strictly speaking this is determined by the metre of the song. More detail on this can be found in Appendix 2.

When leading a choir or group they need to know which note to come in on. This can be done by singing the 'count-in' on the first note of the song. But when performing to others the count-in is intrusive so having a little introduction in peferable. This could be the last phrase of the verse played on a recorder and it will remind children of the link between the verses when they will come in automatically.

If you have learnt a few chords on the guitar you can use the strumming introduction as a way of giving children the beat but you will still need to count to bring them in together. Usually they will pick up the note from the guitar chord so long as they have tried it out a few times. The guitar is a very handy instrument to accompany children singing. While playing you can face the children and, if you know the chords well, maintain good eye contact with the group.

Children leading

It is a very important aspect of music education that children have opportunities to lead. These can be very simple roles such as leading a composing activity within a small group. It could also be taking over the role of leading the class from the teacher. An activity such as 'Have you brought your singing voice' from Chapter 1 is one that a teacher will lead initially but when the children know it well, one of the class can come to the front and take over the teacher's role by thinking of their own different kinds of voices. You will be able to think of children you have met in school who would respond very readily to this opportunity. These are the children who may be attention-seeking and here is an opportunity to turn this motivation to good use.

Children as time-keepers

Time-keeping is another valuable role that children can take on in a performance. Their role is to maintain a steady pulse. One way to do this is to direct the child to walk on the spot and to keep time with their feet on a drum or a wood block. An interesting extension to this is to have a group of four children create a count of four by each playing a different instrument in a cycle.

PRACTICAL TASK PRACTICAL TASK PRACTICAL TASK PRACTICAL TASK PRACTICAL TASK

Test your own ability to keep a steady beat by tapping a pulse on a tin can with a pen in time to your feet as you walk around the room.

Classroom organisation for instrumental activities

Organisation for instrumental work is critical.

REFLECTIVE TASK

Learning objective: To think about how to organise a music lesson with behaviour management in mind.

Apply some of the principles of class and behaviour management that you have learnt about in other contexts to this practical activity. Consider how each principle can be applied in a music lesson using instruments.

Some of these might be:

- structure of the lesson;
- children understanding the purpose of a lesson;
- movement being carefully managed;
- all children being purposefully employed;
- establishing rules early on.

Clearly a lesson which is based on routines and well established rules of behaviour will run more smoothly. For those of you teaching music for the first time, try to base organisation on routines that have been established in other lessons. However, you will need some specific forms of organisation in addition. One of these will be the expectation that children only play instruments when directed to. A simple way to do this is to have a signal or sign. This could be a card with green for GO on one side and red for STOP on the other. This arrangement is very effective when the class is performing or for periods of improvisation.

Below is an example of a lesson that exemplifies a range of organisational points. In this case I have included a simultaneous commentary.

Teaching example

Description	Commentary

Lesson objective: to understand how music can express character.
Resources:
 	
  Animal picture cards
  Three trays of instruments
  IWB	

A class of children sit in a circle. The teacher distributes one card to each child. In the centre of the circle are the three trays of instruments. The children are seated in five groups of five. The teacher invites all children to think of the type of instrument with which to play a sound that will suggest the character of the animal.	Seating children in a circle facilitates organisation of grouping and resources. The teacher prepares children so that they don't waste time.
The teacher then sets a timer on the interactive whiteboard and directs the first group to choose an instrument each. The children each choose an instrument, carry it quietly back to their place and place it on the floor in front of where they are seated before the time runs out. When all the groups have instruments the teacher directs the class to take a minute to try out ways of playing the instrument. She says, *I want you to find two different kinds of sound*. She then shows a green card, after which the children experiment with sound-making. One or two appear to be making noise indiscriminately. The teacher shows the class a red card. The teacher has seen one child who has shown care in his exploring and asks the child to demonstrate his sounds and he plays a series of long and short sounds on a tambourine. The teacher asks the child which animal is being portrayed. He says, 'kangaroo'. The teacher asks the class why the sound reminds them of a kangaroo. A number of hands go up	A timer or a little chant is often useful to speed up choosing time. The teacher sets a time for the activity so that the children are kept focused. The children have clear routines for managing instruments. These include recognising a green sign for 'pick up instruments and play' and a red sign for 'stop playing'. The teacher is monitoring to see which children are being most successful and those that are not so that she can then give the children a model of successful working. The teacher in praising the child reinforces the objective of the lesson that the music should illustrate the character of the animal.

and the teacher chooses one because the child is often rather reluctant to participate. The child says, *The music bounces along like a kangaroo.* The child is praised and the teacher points out that the sound has a pattern to it that makes it special to the animal. She then gives more time for the class to refine their sounds.	She uses this opportunity to encourage any more reticent or reluctant members of the class.

Storage

Storage should not be so complicated that a large part of the lesson is taken up with retrieval and putting away. Instruments kept on a trolley in trays which have broad classifications are very accessible (see Figure 8.1).

Figure 8.1 Instrument storage with diagrams to make classifications clear

The trays can be removed from a trolley and placed nearer to the children during a lesson so that the movement involved in choosing instruments is minimised. For younger children, having places on a trolley that are the shape of the instrument can be very helpful and this can then also be labelled with the name of the instrument. This arrangement establishes good habits and reinforces the knowledge of names. The only difficulty is that it takes up more space.

Teaching strategies and their organisation

Taking turns and circle games

Taking turns games enable children to have some creative input while being aware of others and all of that within a structured activity. An example might be children seated in a circle and each having an instrument on the floor in front of them. The teacher directs all to pick up instruments quietly. She directs them to copy a rhythm she plays. Once this is learnt she instructs them to play all together followed by each child in turn playing their own improvised rhythm. The pattern is carried on round the circle.

In line with good practice in the teaching of other subjects and in the 'Breadth of Study' aspect of the National Curriculum, music lessons should include a variety of forms of organisation. Much of the input aspect of a lesson may require the teacher in a leading role. However, it is important that children have opportunities to develop skills and to consolidate their understanding through small group activity. The following activity is an example of how this may be organised within a whole-class session.

Teaching example

The teacher organises the class into a wide semicircle with the children paired up (or sitting with their talking partners). She reads the poem (below) once and then starts a second time and this time she allocates an answer line to each pair, e.g. 'gold and money', 'The mousie's run away with it', etc. The teacher talks about and demonstrates how the children can choose instruments because of their particular timbre and how they can play them in a particular way, e.g. fast or slow or loud and quiet. There is a rule she gives them to make the task more demanding. She says that the music should accompany all of the words and that both instruments should be used, sometimes separately and at least once together. There are trays of instruments inside the circle and the teacher directs sets of three or four pairs at a time to choose the instruments they want to use. When all the class have instruments they are given five minutes to create their musical accompaniment. The performance of the resulting piece is organised as if in a recording studio using a cassette or digital recorder, with the use of red and green cards to manage the class noise. The teacher reads out the question lines and the pairs of children respond. Later the recording is used to appraise the resulting performance.

Burnie's Hill

What's in there?	Where's the water?
Gold and money	The brown bull drank it.
Where's my share?	Where's the brown bull?
The mousie's run away with it	Back of Burnie's Hill.
Where's the mousie?	Where's Burnie's Hill?
In his housie.	All clad in snow.
Where's his housie?	Where's the snow?
In the wood.	The sun melted it.
Where's the wood?	Where's the sun?
The fire's burnt it.	Way, way up in the air.
Where's the fire?	
The water's quenched it.	

Call and response

Any call-and-response activity is useful for introducing a musical idea. Although its origins are in work songs it has become a standard music teaching strategy. This is in effect is rote learning and it is highly effective if the learning is essentially memorising.

Boom a chick a boom

CALL	RESPONSE
Boom a chick a boom	Boom a chick a boom
I said boom a chick a boom	Boom a chick a boom

I said boom a chick a rock a chick a
               rock a chick a boom
	Boom a chick a rock a chick a
	               rock a chick a boom

Ah ha	Ah ha
Oh yeah!	Oh yeah!

One more time
Real loud

One more time
Real loud

For each new verse, repeat the verse above but in a different kind of voice. In the last line of each verse there is a new instruction to explore as many different ways of chanting. Use as full a range of musical elements as possible:

Timbre – like a robot, operatic, real posh
Dynamics – real quiet, real loud
Pace, tempo – real fast, real slow

And so on until the final repeat might be 'real cool' and end with 'one more time...no way!'

This strategy is more often used for learning songs but can also be very effective for teaching rhythm patterns or opening up the possibility of creative responses. For instance, the teacher might start with an echoing activity such as the rhythm game 'Follow me' that we met in Chapter 1 (p11) and then use the same technique when the children have all got instruments. This could then develop into the teacher calling a name followed by playing a rhythm and the child playing an answering rhythm back.

This activity can lead on naturally to a child taking over the leading role. There is then the potential for the class to be divided into small groups of about four. One of the group can take on the lead role and the others respond. This maximises the opportunities for leading and creates children who can be more active and responsible for themselves. But also the teacher can take the time to observe how children have understood or are demonstrating skills.

We have often referred to the organisation of the class in a circle or horseshoe for music lessons. It will have become apparent that this is very convenient for organisational purposes. See Figure 8.2.

Figure 8.2 Class organisation

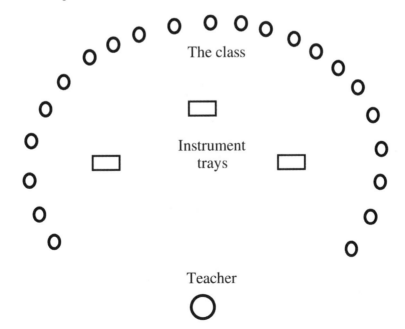

The teacher and children can see each other clearly. Not only can the teacher talk to the children and lead them, but the children can perform or talk to each other. Implicit in the arrangement is a particular kind of teaching that raises what children say or perform to one another to a level of importance alongside what the teacher communicates to them. If a musical game is being played, there may well be a need for a full circle (Figure 8.3). The teacher sings a question to the child on his right:

g　　　　g g　　　g　　g
　　e　e　　　e　　　　　　e

'My name is Mister Jones. What's your name?

The activity progresses round the circle. The teacher can play a simple accompaniment of repeated g and e as an ostinato which all the children can see. In turn the children sing and all the others can echo the name and see each other as they respond.

Figure 8.3 Full circle

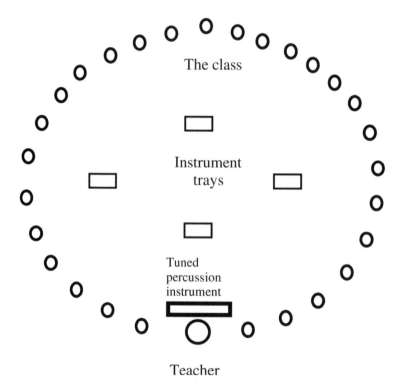

If later in the lesson instruments were to be introduced as in the animal picture activity earlier in this chapter, the children can access the instruments in the trays without undue moving about. As the children move within the circle it keeps movement in the direct sight of the teacher all the time.

Games that require passing an idea round are much clearer to children in this arrangement than if they are sitting in a random group on the carpet. Also splitting into small groups can be managed very quickly by counting out as the teaching moves round the circle.

The circle is very effective for organising groups of children taking on different musical roles. Then when they perform, each part will come from a different direction which adds the effect of antiphony (stereo). Quite a simple effect would be singing the song from Chapter 6 (p94) called 'Tongo', which is sung in two parts echoing each other across the circle.

Planning

Like physical education, music has a place both in and outside the curriculum. As we have seen throughout this book, it may find a place for itself as part of other subject teaching, it may be an aid to organisation or it may be a feature of whole school events.

First let us look at how these elements can fit together.

PRACTICAL TASK PRACTICAL TASK PRACTICAL TASK PRACTICAL TASK PRACTICAL TASK

In Chapter 1 there was a practical task that asked you to log where in the school day you encountered particular musical activities. Now, after having given more thought and accumulated more experience and when you have experienced at least one continuous week in school, make a log of where and when music has occurred and follow this by analysing the activity in terms of how it contributes to musical learning and record on the grid below. There is an example to start you off.

Remember to include the musical categories of listening to recorded music, singing and playing regardless of whether you consider it to be 'performance' or not, as well as any creative music-making.

Activity	Performing	Composing	Appraising	Listening
Music as children come into classroom				Quiet listening music. Aids classroom atmosphere. Some knowledge of the music but no knowledge or understanding about music.

From the task it will be apparent how the music curriculum has to be accounted for in a range of places and times. This should be reflected in the medium-term planning (a unit of work) for music teaching. For instance, if the music listening before assembly is discussed at some point and the name of the music is displayed, then the curriculum purpose of listening is partly fulfilled. The component that appears to be missing is the appraisal aspect in which the children are able to respond to the music and share their understanding in some way. However, it might be that in a dance lesson they were asked to respond in their movement to the character of some music. Then they will have been appraising in quite a different way and the two musical activities will complement each other. But at the heart of all the music provision will be class music lessons and it is these that give coherence to the children's experience of music at school.

A unit of work

Sequence and progression
Much of each lesson in a unit of work lasting half a term will be taken up with learning a few songs, developing a composing technique, or refining rhythm games. Therefore necessarily

there needs to be repetition from lesson to lesson with gradual refinement and increasing demands being made. This may be in the techniques the children use but may also be in their use of the subject specific language, e.g. rhythm, melody, pulse, and so on. Songs need to be learnt comfortably by heart. Finger play or larger movements aid memory and add another dimension. Composing activities need to develop, a little added to the task each time, but occasionally a simpler task needs to be revisited for consolidation.

See Appendix 1 for an example of a unit of work template.

A music lesson

Each lesson should contain a variety of activities drawing on the four activities: composing, performing (both singing and instrumental) and listening and appraising. But also a number of routines will help to establish good habits.

The intended outcomes of the lesson
The learning objectives need to be set out for the children. Be careful to think about what children are learning from the activities they undertake. What skills, knowledge or understanding will they have gained from the activity?

- They may have an increased repertoire of songs or knowledge of pieces of music.
- They may develop specific skills.
- But also they may have more understanding of the elements that constitute music, i.e. pitch, duration, dynamics, tempo, timbre, texture or structure.

Warm-up activities
These will often be short whole-class activities simply to focus the children's attention and to warm up their voices.

Introductory activities
These activities are for developing skills and understandings required in the main activity. Usually this will be a teacher-led activity with the whole group. However, include opportunities for children to demonstrate and to lead activities. The following are the broad activity areas with one or two examples. In one lesson you will focus on one area.

Singing activities (not only songs):

- limited pitch singing (singing names and simple rhymes to two or three notes);
- exploring the voice (loud/soft, slow/fast, articulation, character, varying manners of performance).

Rhythm games:

- call and response;
- taking turns round a circle.

Composing games:

- using grids as graphic score frameworks;
- using grids to create rhythmic patterns to a regular pulse;
- use of cards with pictures and words to suggest rhythm patterns.

Main activities

Performing

- Stimulating ways of learning a song by ear by singing in different ways, developing an inner voice (missing out notes and phrases in songs).
- Simple instrumental accompaniments (drones and ostinati for harmony – untuned percussion for rhythm and timbre).

Composing

- Games involving inventing rhythms.
- Sound stories or pictures.
- Group composition in twos, threes, or fours.
- Making or working from graphic scores.

Listening

- Listening to recorded music in an active way – consider what activity (either physical or mental) children can do while listening.
- Consider the range of listening material drawn from contemporary and historical sources, from the Western tradition and other world music traditions.

Plenary – evaluation and conclusion

This is the opportunity for children to appraise their own work. They can be guided to appraise or evaluate performances of songs or compositions within the lesson. This may include recording or making a graphic score of a composition. Try to arrange some opportunities for the children to perform to other children or adults in other venues from time to time. Perhaps you will conclude with a well-known song for the pleasure of singing together and creating a sense of well-being in the class.

General planning issues

Timing

The recommendation for Early Years is for music lessons to be about 20 to 30 minutes. A little quite often is preferable. For later years, 30 to 50 minutes is recommended.

Resources

Have all instruments ready to hand but preferably in trays which children can collect from and return. Consider variety but have a clear focus to your choice, i.e. a focus on timbre will require a variety of interesting instrumental timbres, metal, wood, shakers, electronic keyboard and so on. Have any recording equipment within arm's length.

Observation and assessment

Assessment in music is similar to assessment in PE. The teacher is very active and will find it difficult to recall individual accomplishments unless the observation is focused. In the first instance you need to think about the connection between teacher observation and appraisal. We encourage children to listen critically to the work they undertake as it develops as well as evaluating the final product. That is in essence what is meant by appraisal and that is what we should do as teachers as well. Hence there are only two key forms of assessment:

- monitoring of activity and immediate feedback (assessment for learning);
- summative appraisal (assessment of learning).

In many other subjects you are likely to have a set of pieces of work to mark at the end of a lesson but in performance subjects this is unusual. On-the-spot appraisal is much more effective and so even if you or the children do make recordings these are better used in the lesson. However, you may have graphic scores to look at after the lesson.

I would suggest that you plan to focus on the work of three children in the class during the lesson, so that if you are leading a song you will notice the degree to which these children are participating. While singing together this is all that can be noted. But if there is follow-up activity in small groups you will be able to note whether they are being successful in the task much more accurately. For instance, if the children are doing a whole-class call-and-response song based on the notes *g* and *e* the objective will be to increase the children's accuracy in pitch.

Teacher: *g*   *g*   Children: *g*   *g*
              e   *e*   *e*   *e*
      Who's got black hair?   I've got black hair

Subgroups of children will respond to a sung question and the teacher will be able to hear the level of success of individual children.

PRACTICAL TASK PRACTICAL TASK PRACTICAL TASK PRACTICAL TASK PRACTICAL TASK

In a singing activity similar to the one above, it is useful to think of the range of possible responses:

1. silence;

2. speaking;

3. singing on one note;

4. singing on two notes – high then low but not the same ones as the teacher;

5. singing two notes accurately;

6. singing two notes accurately and confidently.

When listening to a small group or an individual child singing, see if you can locate the responses of the children or child on this scale.

It may be that the achievement of one or two children not identified for assessment will stand out and so their responses can be recorded as well. In each lesson the children being observed will be different and so over a period of time the whole class can be covered.

As in all teaching, monitoring is also important in maintaining the success and pace of the lesson. You have to consider whether the level of success is great enough to move on or if there is a need for revisiting the skill. If the mood of the lesson is buoyant then one can challenge more and press for higher level work. Being able to hear these levels of achievement in a variety of musical activities will grow with experience. Try to break the lesson objectives down in the way that the singing activity was. At least try to go beyond *they joined in/they didn't join in*. It will require some musical knowledge of course. For instance, if the lesson is focused on dynamics you will be listening for whether the children do play or sing both quietly and loudly to achieve particular effects. If the children are creating compositions in groups the appraisal plenary session at the end will give you plenty of evidence. Try to plan the children's groups ahead so that you can have them written down on an assessment sheet. Then you can just jot down a word or two. Even in group performances it is a good idea to have focus children that you observe in more detail.

Planning for learning difficulties

In Chapter 1 we wrote about the inclusive musical classroom. Here I will look at the specific needs of particular conditions that children with learning difficulties may have and how these may be accommodated.

To begin with, here is a story that underlines the importance of inclusion in mainstream classrooms for some children with learning difficulties.

CLASSROOM STORY

This story relates to a child with quite severe behavioural, emotional and social difficulties that manifested, for instance, in temper tantrums associated with making errors in mathematics. However, she decided that she would like to learn to play the recorder and she joined the lunchtime class. She worked hard at learning the descant recorder and progressed well and after not long she began to learn the treble recorder as well. Throughout this period her emotional outbursts decreased and she began to manage sustained periods of concentrated learning in the classroom. Moreover, at home she had begun to be not only accepted around her home estate but to be respected for her achievement.

REFLECTIVE TASK

Learning objective: To clarify the relationship between learning in music and in other subjects.

For the child in the previous classroom story, making errors while working at mathematics set off temper tantrums but making errors while practising the recorder did not. Consider what was so different about these different activities and how music may have contributed to the emotional development of this child. Is this type of learning experience unique to music? Is it that the experience is therapeutic or is it a different kind of learning?

Might a teacher learn something from the way such a child's learning happens or, perhaps, the nature of what is to be learnt that would enable the child to access other subjects more easily?

Bearing in mind therefore that you will be working with children in your classes with a range of learning difficulties these five general headings identified by Lois Birkenshaw will be helpful:

1. *Group participation*
2. *Speech production*
3. *Learning basic skills and concepts*
4. *Movement*
5. *Relaxation*
(1974, p313)

1. The social aspects of musical activities are very important for children who have become withdrawn. This is one way of interacting with other children without the challenge and unpredictability of other social activities. The structure of the music provides safety and boundaries that will encourage such children. The governing force of a performance is seen as non-human and thus easier for children with behavioural, emotional and social difficulties (BESD) to comply with. The notion of taking turns is driven by a place in the music and stopping must happen at the end of a song. These are strong social learning opportunities for children with such difficulties and particularly those with autistic spectrum disorders.

2. Even ordinary speech patterns have a rhythm to them. The way names are said will have stresses in particular places and a flow that makes them sound the same every time they are said. You will notice how extending one syllable distorts the sound and may make a name unrecognisable (hence the incomprehensibility of some opera and pop song lyrics) and so the rhythm is important to the development of speech. Use of rhymes with strong rhythms such as those in Chapter 3 and as follows, will meet the needs of all children.

Bow wow wow,
Whose dog art thou?
Little Tommy Tinker's dog
Bow wow wow.

The flow of the lines when spoken out loud and preferably from memory will often enable children to overcome stutters and voluntary mutism. This effect is enhanced by the accompaniment of instruments keeping time. Holding up cards with the key words will help with reading skills also.

3. A focus on basic skills will be to the benefit of all children but those with learning difficulties need this more than most. Bean and Oldfield (1991) have set out a range of games to develop such basic skills in children. For developing listening skills the main theme is that children should respond with a specific action when they hear specific sounds. It may be that the pitch is specific, as in the game 'Which Way?' The teacher plays on an electric keyboard and the children are seated in a circle. When the music starts, a set of bells is passed around the circle. When the teacher plays two particularly high notes the bells must be passed in the reverse direction. For social awareness a game such as 'Hello' is effective. The teacher uses an instrument such as a guiro to say *hello* to individual children, who it is hoped will say, *hello* in reply. Some more reluctant ones may be given an instrument to reply with. Such games can also develop physical skills such as passing a so-called sleeping tambourine around a circle so carefully that it does not wake up.

The use of music to help memorise information has been covered to an extent already in Chapter 7 but here you will need to consider how many sets of key ideas can be learnt by chanting or singing.

- Days of the week and months of the year are often used as skipping chants.
- Colours can be listed in a song.
- Numbers may be counted up to a rhythm and multiples sung in a song.

4. Using music as a stimulus for movement has been a feature of this book in Chapters 2 and 6. However, it can be overlooked that musical games and songs can contribute to very basic body awareness. The most obvious of these would be 'Heads and shoulders knees and toes', which you last encountered in French in Chapter 7. The vigorous actions in this song help to keep children engaged but above all the coincidence of the kinaesthetic, the aural and the visual by touching the body part with the singing of its name will ensure these are remembered. Other songs that fit into this category are:

'Do the Hokey Cokey'
'If you're happy and you know it'
'Little cabin in a wood'
'One finger one thumb keep moving'
'Tommy thumb'

Many songs also help to develop spatial awareness by involving dance patterns or illustrative movements that use either just the fingers or the whole body.

'Here we go round the mulberry bush'
'Two fat gentlemen met in a lane' [finger play starting with thumbs]
'Oats and beans and barley grow'
'Dingle dangle scarecrow'

(all songs found in *This Little Puffin*)

Most of the movement songs mentioned above are suited to younger children. However, there are songs with strong movements that are suited to older children such as 'Heads and shoulders baby'.

The children stand in a circle, each with a partner. They turn to face their partner.

Both hands touch head shoulders then clap in front
Singing: Heads and shoulders baby

Right hand crosses over to clap right of the partner
Singing: One,

Left hand crosses over to clap left of the partner
Singing: two,

Both hands clap those of the partner
Singing: three

5. For general vocal warm-up activities which enable children to relax, refer to the relevant section of Chapter 3.

Extra-curricular music

This section is mainly for information rather than instruction, because the National Curriculum requirements for teaching music do not include extra-curricular activities. However, there is also a recognition that many of you with an interest in music will participate in extra-curricular musical events and clubs and this will then contribute to your demonstration of professionalism as described in Standard 3(b), which requires trainees to *be aware of the policies and practices of the workplace and share in collective responsibility for their implementation*. These general practices include lunchtime or after-school clubs and it is these clubs and activities that this section will focus on.

In order to understand where these activities fit into the expectations that the British public has of primary education, we need to go back a little in time because unlike primary schools in other European countries, in Britain there has always been an expectation that teachers take responsibility for more than the curriculum. Teachers supervise on the playground, they have a concern for the general welfare of children and they run activities for children that extend the curriculum. There have been periods when teachers have felt exploited and have withdrawn the goodwill that makes most of this possible but in the early years of the 2000s, partly because of the relative good pay, teachers have been willing to extend the school day. It is also acknowledged that all of these roles come under the framework of Every Child Matters, for which schools have accepted a responsibility. The *Music Manifesto* of 2004 records that the government in 2000 had pledged that *over time, all pupils in primary schools who wished to, would have the opportunity to learn an instrument*. This was to be supported by the Wider Opportunities programme for children at Key Stage 2. A pilot project was set up and the government then allocated further funding to be used to support the work throughout the country. The pilot identified *the involvement of more musicians and teachers with increased higher quality training*, among other factors in order for such work to be sustained. The training at a higher level to support such professionals was begun in the year 2007/8. With this beginning to fall into place, the *Music Manifesto* had further recommendations, among which are the following.

1. All Foundation Stage and Key Stage 1 pupils have opportunities for regular whole-class and whole-school singing.
2. By 2010, every Key Stage 2 pupil should be able to experience at least one year of enhanced National Curriculum music, including an extended period of whole-class or large-group instrumental and voice tuition.
3. The government report on the progress of Key Stage 2 music entitlement by September 2008.
4. Continued support to extend and broaden the opportunities to be offered to talented children through local arrangements for gifted and talented children.

The *Music Manifesto* goes on to say that *music has a particularly important role to play in the lives of vulnerable and at risk children, and those with special needs*. But the Manifesto team recognises that such children were poorly served at the time of the Second Report in 2006 and has recommendations to move this provision forward.

Where does extra-curricular music fit in?

Instrumental music lessons

In the mix of activities we hope there will be some group or individual instrumental lessons. These are likely to take place in extra-curricular time but may be during other lessons and, if so, children are withdrawn. At present it is unlikely that all children in a school will be having instrumental lessons. But if the ambitions of the *Music Manifesto* are realsed there will be universal opportunities for children to take part in group or class lessons on instruments that are now only available to some. The kind of instruments available will depend on what a local authority or music organisation offers but most commonly you will encounter the following taught in group or individual lessons.

- Recorder group – either all descant or a mixture to include treble and tenor.
- Guitar group.
- Steel pans – taught as a band.
- Electric keyboards – group teaching.
- Orchestral instruments – most often started in groups.
  - violin, viola, cello;
  - clarinet, flute, saxophone;
  - trumpet, trombone.
- Brass band instruments:
  - cornet;
  - tenor horn;
  - euphonium and baritone;
  - trombone.

Some local authorities or schools specialise in a range of world musics including African drumming, samba band, and Indian music. I know of one small school where most of the children learn to play the mandolin and a large school where balalaika classes are an option. Some schools do have piano teaching on offer but this is difficult to organise on a group basis.

There are other instruments that are not so popular or may have particular demands that mean they need to be taken up when children are older. These include the string and brass bass, the oboe and bassoon.

School choirs and bands

School choirs or singing groups are the musical equivalent of school teams in games. However, often at primary level there is no selection as there may be for games teams. Selection is a subject of some debate. In some schools where there are plenty of opportunities for children to demonstrate their skills, selection will give a boost to those with musical talent but where the only chance of singing well is in the choir, selection may have the effect of putting children off singing.

The children may be lucky enough to have a band organised by an enthusiastic teacher. The attainment of the children will determine whether they are able to take part. So it is quite possible to be selective about who takes part by having a policy that any child who reaches a certain standard may join. However, there is plenty of music written inclusively to accommodate a wide range of abilities.

RESEARCH SUMMARY RESEARCH SUMMARY **RESEARCH SUMMARY** RESEARCH SUMMARY

Peter Cope (Dept of Education University of Stirling)

Paper given at BERA annual conference 1997

Cope looks at the assumptions that lie behind the choice of musical genres and styles that form the basis of school instrumental tuition. He challenges the use of repertoire drawn from the classical tradition that forms the majority of material used to train children in instrumental music. He gives emphasis to the importance of social contexts of music-making that the majority of children will enjoy at home or that their parents would enjoy. He argues that in Scotland learning the fiddle and using jigs and reels as the repertoire makes a much more worthwhile experience. It contrasts with children who by learning the viola, for instance, find that they only have one option for their music-making, which is in an orchestra whose repertoire they and their parents may find unfamiliar. One primary school known to the author has a fiddle group that has no formal teaching but has generated independent practice groups who meet three times a week. He feels that tuning into the local cultural context has made the music a far more meaningful and rewarding experience for the children involved.

School performances

An important part of school life is the yearly performance. This may be associated with festivals or may be placed pragmatically at the end of the summer term when all tests are safely put away. However, more modest occasions such as Friday morning assembly will also be an opportunity for performance which will give more meaning and purpose to the weekly lessons and daily practice. Music will always form a significant part of such occasions. These are the times in the school when the community aspect of music is brought to the fore.

CASE STUDY

An overview of extra-curricular music in one school

Delph village has a history of brass band music. It is only right therefore that the local primary school nurtures this in its pupils. Delph Primary School has a very strong and recognised tradition of providing peripatetic music lessons for brass instruments. Children begin in Year 3 and receive lessons every week from a brass teacher based at the Oldham Music Centre. As soon as the children achieve an appropriate level of proficiency, they are invited to play in the school's brass band, which currently has 20 or so members. The band play at school events and at regular intervals on the school calendar. They also go on 'tour' at Christmas, visiting a link school, in the centre of Oldham and also to the local retirement home. At Christmas the band play in the village square accompanied by carollers.

As well as the brass musicians the school also has a string contingent with children ranging from Year 1 to Year 6. There are currently about 15 violinists and six cellists. As with the brass band, these musicians perform for various events in the school calendar. The school has recently added a summer concert to its events diary and this gives all the musicians, and pupils generally, the chance to celebrate their achievements.

There is also a choir that is currently around 40 strong that children from Year 4 upwards can join. All the musicians participate in the annual Music Festival in Oldham along with many schools of both primary and secondary age.

If some of these activities take place in your placement school then it will only be some children who opt to join the group or they may be selected by whether parents can or are prepared to pay. This accounts for its exclusion from the National Curriculum. However, if the ambitions of the *Music Manifesto* are fully realised we may see the time when it will be considered part of every child's entitlement. Some schools have already made use of Wider Opportunities funding to offer this entitlement to all the children in their school.

CASE STUDY

Every child a brass instrument player

In another part of the Oldham authority, St Hugh's C of E Primary School, led by their head teacher, has taken a radical approach to music education. Using the principles of the Wider Opportunities Initiative supported by the Oldham Music Centre, they have worked for four years to enable every child in Key Stage 2 to now play a brass instrument. The lessons are whole class and fully integrated into the curriculum. One lesson each week is dedicated to brass playing but one other delivers general National Curriculum music with a full range of musical activities combined with the brass playing. As an opportunity for more advanced players, there is a school brass band of 35 players and many parents and staff members also play in the band.

Behind this immense musical commitment are principles that go far beyond the music itself. These include:

- opportunities to play instruments should not be decided by whether parents can pay;
- brass playing rather than strings or other wind instrumental playing reflects a regional musical tradition;
- inclusion of parents and staff and parental support for performances at school and further afield have contributed strongly to the school's role as a positive force for raising the self-esteem of both children and the community as a whole;
- brass playing has improved the health of children, particularly those with asthma;
- it is believed that substantial musical activity has contributed to higher mathematical attainment in the school.

The school also has a strong commitment to singing in every class and has a school choir for which children are selected.

One interesting point you will have noted about the musical organisation within St. Hugh's is that extra-curricular and curriculum music have been thoroughly integrated.

Integrating children's musical skills in music lessons

For integration to happen, extra-curricular music activity needs to be taken into account by the generalist class teacher. Children in your class may have particular skills that can be nurtured and made useful by being added to class music-making. There are a number of different levels at which the skills can operate so that teachers with little as well as those with more musical knowledge may successfully integrate these skills into their lessons.

At one level children with more skill in singing, for instance, will raise the game for all the children by setting a standard. In music this is most easily done because it is so public. Performance, after all, is the aural equivalent of wall display and this is one way that teachers demonstrate high standards to the whole class. Singing is a musical skill all the children can develop. However, integrating instrumental players may be less easy to manage. When a song has an introduction, recorder players can often pick this up quite quickly. Some song books will include notated parts for recorders to accompany the singers. The song 'Chu ah ai' from China, met in Chapter 7, has a simple three-note introduction,

as does 'Its raining its pouring', which starts:

Sometimes the part may be more difficult than this but still quite within the capabilities of one or two members of the class. This may be the case for the following, taken from the song 'The Armada', also met in Chapter 7.

If this is so, then a good arrangement is to give the written music to the players a few days before the lesson so that they can prepare it. If they are unsure of the rhythm, for instance, they can ask their recorder teacher for help. Otherwise you will often be relying on accompaniment audio CDs for the children to sing to. Most recorder players can pick up the tune on their instrument from an audio CD in the same way that they can as singers, but they will need preparation time.

It is good for children who may be learning in quite a formal way, with a focus on written notation to join a classroom ensemble. There may be opportunities to play along by ear or to improvise which could be quite new ways of playing. The violin teacher Shinichi Suzuki recognised the importance of instrumentalists listening to their inner ear (Suzuki, 1969). He advocated children as young as four beginning to learn the violin and to learn by ear. Only when they had a good ear for the sound and a good general technique would they learn to read music. In addition it is good for such children to play socially and to combine with other children playing on a variety of instruments.

A SUMMARY OF KEY POINTS

> Leading a performance means giving the class a note to start to sing on, the speed (tempo) and exactly when to start so that all start together.

> There are many opportunities for children to lead in music-making.

> Musical activities should include opportunities for groups as well as the whole class and can include: call and response, echoing, taking turns and circle games.

> Classroom instrumental activities need careful planning and classroom organisation to minimise unnecessary movement and noise.

> The integration of children with special needs in music lessons requires planning and resourcing.

> Extra-curricular music activities have a special contribution to children's musical development and to the school community through concerts and other performances.

> You will have considered how children's musical skills gained in extra-curricular activities can be integrated in to classroom music-making.

Finally, to leave you with an important message particularly related to the section about individual learning needs but with a wider application, here is a story that reminds us of the power of music for all children.

CLASSROOM STORY

In B's classroom there is a child with autistic spectrum disorder. Although in some cases such children will become over-stimulated and upset by the impact of loud musical activities, Sam enjoys and is highly responsive to music as well as having quite a fine singing voice. Another aspect of music is that it evokes emotional responses and children with autistic disorders find emotions difficult to interpret even within themselves. Sam has full-time individual support in a mainstream classroom and on the day of the school Christmas performance he is sitting with his support assistant listening to another class sing a carol while waiting for his turn to sing. The carol is a less well-known one in a minor key and in a gentle, lyrical style. Sam sits absorbed by the performance. His support assistant turns to him to check on him as she so often does but this time she notices tears trickling down H's face. At the end of the song Sam struggles to explain his feelings and says to his assistant, 'Sam's sad.' 'Do you want to go out?' She asks. 'No, no, no!' he answers adamantly.

REFERENCES REFERENCES **REFERENCES** REFERENCES **REFERENCES** REFERENCES

Bean, J. and Oldfield, A. (1991) *Pied Piper*. Cambridge: Cambridge University Press

Birkenshaw, L. (1974) *Music for fun – Music for learning*. Ontario, Canada: Rinehart and Winston

Cope, P. (1997) *Maximising participation in musical instrument playing*. Presented at the British Educational Research Association, 11 September 1997

Matterson, E. (1969) *This little puffin – Finger plays and nursery games*. London: Penguin

Suzuki, S. (1969) (trans. Suzuki, W.) *Nurtured by love: A new approach to education.* Smithtown, NY: Exposition Press

Glossary

Words included in this glossary are here to answer possible questions that may arise as you read the book. They are not all necessary for competent teaching of music in the primary school. However, those marked with an asterisk are the priority terms.

*Accompaniment This is everything in a performance that is not the tune. The support for a tune, usually on lower instruments, which provides rhythm mood and character.

Ambient A contemporary term used to describe music with, generally, calm atmosphere or composed to create a mood.

Antiphony Music sounding from different directions to create stereo effects. Generally this would be two choirs facing each other across a large space singing echoing or answering phrases.

*Appraising Evaluating and judging. This is the consideration of the qualities of a piece of music whether composed by a child or by others.

*Chord This is a set of notes sounded together. A simple major chord of C comprises the notes C, E and G. The chord of A minor comprises A, C and E.

*Classical music This is the term commonly used to describe music composed as an art form, i.e. seen as serious in intent. But technically the term 'classical' describes music that has strict formal qualities associated with art forms of the late eighteenth century.

*Composing The process of creating and notating or recording music.

Consonance and dissonance This is the quality of the relationship between notes sounded together. Consonant sounds are harmonious and dissonant sounds clash.

Dance music In contemporary use the term implies music with a strong, regular beat. Traditionally it is a folk music form which varies in style according to the dance it accompanies, e.g. jig, reel or square dance.

*Drone a simple accompaniment comprising two or three notes held down continuously. This can be heard accompanying a bagpipe melody.

*Elements of music

- Pitch – high and low, melody
- Duration – short and long notes, pulse (or beat), and rhythm
- Dynamics – loud/quiet/silent
- Tempo – fast and slow
- Timbre – tone, the way instruments are played or types of sound
- Texture – the layers of music, the way sounds are combined
- Structure – the way sounds are organised in time

Eurhythmics This is a method of learning to perform music, devised by the Swiss musician Emil Dalcroze, that develops musicality through whole body movement often with simple play equipment such as balls and hoops.

*Graphic score a free-form notation system using invented lines and shapes to suggest, rather then precisely indicate, musical elements.

Improvisation The spontaneous creation of music usually against a familiar chord sequence or preset framework of time and set of notes. If improvised music is notated it becomes a composition.

Key The use in a passage of music of a particular set of notes. In music that conforms to the use of keys, i.e. tonal music, there are two types, major (bright sounding) and minor (sad sounding). The lowest of the set of notes gives the key its name, e.g. C major, and serves as a reference point in a melody.

Key signature The set of sharps or flats at the beginning of every stave that indicates which sharps or flats to play in the piece. This indicates the key of the music.

*Listening The technical term used for focused attention to music.

*Melody or tune This is a carefully shaped pattern of pitches and rhythms that plays a dominant part in a composition. The term always implies the inclusion of pitch so that a melody will always have a contour of ups and downs. A rhythm alone is not a melody or tune.

*Metre or count This is the pulse broken down into units (called bars) of simple number counts. The most common is four; three has been common in the past and two is natural for dance and march-like music. More irregular metres such as seven are uncommon but used in some modern music. The Indian classical tradition uses a much greater variety of metres.

Modern music This is the term commonly used to describe contemporary popular forms of music but technically used to describe art music of the twentieth century.

*Notation This is the term for ways of recording music in written form.

- Traditional Western notation records all the music elements in detail.
- Graphic notation uses pictures and a variety of lines and shapes to indicate musical ideas and leaves room for interpretation.

Note values

| Minim | Semibreves | Crotchets | Quavers | (British system) |
| Whole note | Half notes | Quarter notes | Eighth notes | (American system) |

*Ostinato A repeated pattern. Sometimes this is a rhythm but often it is a short tune.

*Pentatonic scale A set of five notes on which to base a composition which is most commonly in classroom music comprising the notes c d e g and a. The scale is common in folk music throughout the world but particularly in Gamelan and the folk music of China and Japan. It is particularly useful for composing in the classroom because however the parts are combined there will never be strong dissonance.

*Percussion The term used for musical instruments that are struck and hence do not have sustained sound.

- **Untuned** – without definite pitch. These instruments may be struck with a beater or the hand, scraped with a stick, or shaken.
- **Tuned** – with definite pitch. Usually made up of a number of sounding bars to make up a scale.

*Performing This is presenting music that has been prepared to any kind of audience large or small.

Phrase A musical sentence. A melody comprises a series of phrases. Often phrases are paired in the form of a question and an answer phrase.

Polyrhythm This is a characteristic of drumming music in which each part or drum has a different rhythmic pattern.

*Pulse The basic beat that determines the tempo. This is the sound of the bass drum in a band.

*Pulse grid Each box represents a single pulse or beat. The number of boxes in each row will match the metre of the piece i.e. how the pulses are grouped in sets of 4, or 3 or 5…

A pulse grid in 4

*Rhythm This is a musical pattern that has no pitch, played on a percussion instrument or on one note.

*Sharps and flats (# and ♭) Generally speaking these are the black notes on the piano. One white note, say D, can be sharpened to D# or flattened to D♭.

*Silent voice (inner voice) This is a useful term to describe hearing music in the head.

Soprano, alto, tenor and bass The names given to higher and lower female and male voices. The same names are often used to describe a set of similar instruments that are basically the same except that they are pitched higher or lower.

*Sound sources Sound-makers, e.g.:

- **Body sounds** – sounds made with the body alone, e.g. clicking fingers, clapping, stamping. However, singing is not usually included as a body sound.

- **Improvised instruments**.
- **Manufactured instruments**.

*Sounds table A table with sound-making equipment or materials on for use by children in Early Years settings.

Stave The set of five lines on which musical notation is set out.

Time signature Numerals at the beginning of a stave of music to indicate the metre of the music (see Appendix 2).

*World musics This is the Eurocentric term used to describe music from non-Western music traditions. Some commentators disagree with the term because they don't find this binary distinction of Western and non-Western musics helpful. Two examples are:

- Gamelan – music of Indonesia;
- Bhangra – dance music from the Punjab (India/Pakistan).

Appendix 1
Lesson or unit of work templates

Highlight the relevant aspects of the National Curriculum and write in the details of the resources and activities in the relevant open spaces.

Music Planning Sheet for lesson/unit of work		Key Stage 1
Teacher	Year Group	Timing

Songs and listening repertoire/instruments and resources

Focus elements:　　　pitch　　duration　　dynamics　　tempo　　timbre　　texture　　structure

1. Performing **controlling sounds** a. sing songs and speak chants expressively b. play tuned and untuned instruments c. rehearse and perform with others	
2 Composing **creating and developing musical ideas** a. create musical patterns b. explore, choose and organise sounds and ideas	
3. Appraising **Responding and reviewing** a. explore and express ideas and feelings about music b. make improvements to their own work	
4. Listening **Applying knowledge and understanding** a. listen with concentration and internalise and recall sounds with increasing aural memory b. how musical elements are used within simple structures c. how sounds are made in different ways d. how music is used for particular purposes	

5. Breadth of study – pupils should be taught the knowledge, skills and understanding through:
a. activities that integrate performing, composing and appraising
b. responding to a range of musical and non-musical starting points
c. working individually, in groups and as a class
d. a range of live and recorded music from different times and cultures

Assessment criteria

Most children will:

Some children will not make so much progress and will:

Some children will have progressed further and will:

Music Planning Sheet for lesson/unit of work		Key Stage 2
Teacher	Year Group	Timing

Songs and listening repertoire/instruments and resources

Focus elements: pitch   duration   dynamics   tempo   timbre   texture   structure

1. Performing
controlling sounds
a. sing unison and two-part songs
b. play tuned and un-tuned instruments
c. rehearse and present performances with awareness of audience

2. Composing
creating and developing musical ideas
a. improvise, developing rhythmic and melodic ideas
b. explore, choose, combine and organise sounds and ideas within musical structures

3. Appraising
Responding and reviewing
a. analyse and compare sounds
b. explore and explain ideas and feelings about music
c. make improvements to their own work

4. Listening
Applying knowledge and understanding
a. listen with attention to detail and internalise and recall sounds with increasing aural memory
b. musical use of elements – how they can be organised within simple structures to create moods and effects
c. how music is produced and notated
d. the influence of time and place on how music is created, performed and heard

5. Breadth of study – pupils should be taught the knowledge, skills and understanding through:
a. activities that integrate performing, composing and appraising
b. responding to a range of musical and non-musical starting points
c. working individually, in groups of different sizes and as a class
d. using ICT to capture, change and combine sounds
e. a range of live and recorded music from different times and cultures

Assessment criteria

Most children will:

Some children will not make so much progress and will:

Some children will have progressed further and will:

Appendix 2
How to count in at the beginning of a song

If a song is in the metre four beats to a bar this will be indicated by a time signature at the beginning of the stave. If the metre is four it will normally be written as 4 over 4. The first 4 indicates how many beats and the 4 underneath indicates what kind of beats, which in this case are quarter notes or crotchets (as they are known in the UK).

This time signature tells us that the count or metre is four crotchets in each bar

So the teacher will count in four beats to start the song.

This time signature indicates three crotchets in a bar.

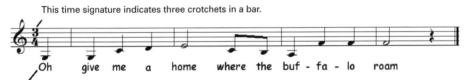

So the teacher will first think of counting in 'one, two, three' but in this song there is an up-beat, a note that anticipates the first bar, on the word 'Oh'. Because beat 'three' is to be sung, the teacher only counts in 'one, two'.

Appendix 3
Additional songs for Chapters 3 and 5

Chapter 3

Call and response song   *Day oh*

A story song   *There was a princess long ago*

And she lived in a big high tower, etc

One day a bad queen cast a spell...

The princess slept for a hundred years...

A great big forest grew around...

A gallant prince came riding by...

He cut the tress down with his sword...

He took her hand to wake her up...

So everybody's happy now..

Partner songs   *A ram sam sam* and *Pease pudding hot*

These tunes can be sung together and combine to make satisfying harmony.

Chapter 5

Teddy Bear, Teddy Bear

Two-note song using g and e (the falling minor third)

g g g   g g
        e e e   e   etc.
Teddy bear, teddy bear, touch the ground,

g g g e e e g g e
Teddy bear, teddy bear, turn around,

g g g e e e g g e
Teddy bear, teddy bear, tie your shoe,

g g g e e e g g e
Teddy bear, teddy bear, that will do.

g g g e e e g g e
Teddy bear, teddy bear, climb the stairs,

g g g e e e g g e
Teddy bear, teddy bear, say your prayers,

g g g e e e g g g e
Teddy bear, teddy bear, turn off the light,

g g g e e e g g e
Teddy bear, teddy bear, say goodnight.

Appendix 4
Resources

School songbooks

Harrop, B. (1976) *Okki-tokki-unga – Action songs for children*. London: A & C Black
Harrop, B. (1980) *Apusskidu – Songs for children*. London: A & C Black

Developing singing and later years resources

Sanderson, A. (1995) *Banana splits – ways into part-singing*. London: A & C Black
Nickol, P. (ed.) (1984) *Juke box*. London: A & C Black
Nicholls, S. (2007) *The song stack – Twenty songs for primary school singers*. Kirkby-in-Ashfield: MES
Gadsby, D. and Harrop, B. (1982) *Flying a round – 88 rounds and partner songs*. London: A & C Black

Songs for assembly

Fearon, S. (2003) *Everyone's singing Lord*. London: A & C Black
Gadsby, D. and Hoggarth, J. *Alleluya 77 songs for thinking people*. London: A & C Black

Developing musical skills resource books

Clark, V. (1991) *High low dolly pepper – developing musical skills with young children*. London: A & C Black
Cotton, M. (2005) *Agogo bells to xylophone – A friendly guide to classroom instruments*. London: A & C Black
Nicholls, S. (1992) *Bobby Shaftoe, clap your hands – Musical fun with new songs from old favourites*. London: A & C Black
Nicholls, S. (1998) *Michael Finnigan, tap your chinigin – Developing music skills with new songs from old favourites*. London: A & C Black
Umansky, K. (1998) *Three Singing Pigs*. London: A & C Black
Umansky, K. (1998) *Three rapping rats – Making music with traditional stories.* London: A & C Black

Cross-curricular resources

Macgregor, H. (1998) *Tom Thumb's musical maths – Developing maths with simple songs*. London: A & C Black
Macgregor, H. (1998) *Bingo lingo – Supporting literacy with songs and rhymes*. London: A & C Black

Computer software

2 simple software – Music Toolkit
Sony Creative software – Super duper looper
Flexi music kids composer. Not as good as Super duper but works on the same principle
Junior Sibelius www.sibelius.com/products

Appendix 5
CD audio recordings

World music

Evening Song (trad.): Jing Ying Soloists – Wotton-under-Edge 1987
The Rough Guide to World Music – London: World Music Network 1994
The Rough Guide to Reggae – London: World Music Network 1995
The Rough Guide to the Music of India – London: World Music Network 1996
The Rough Guide to Salsa – London: World Music Network 1997
The Rough Guide to Irish Music – London: World Music Network 1995
Native American Dream – London: World Music Network 1995
Clan: a Celtic Journey: Medwyn Goodall: New World Music Network 1998
Ben Badoo in *Introduction to World Music* – Womad 2003
Best of African Beats – Bar de Lune Apace music 2007
Ladysmith Black Mambazo – Polygram 1998
Rainforest Dream – Joji Hirota: Saydisc

Historical

Renaissance (fifteenth and sixteenth centuries)
Songs of Chivalry: Martin Best Mediaeval Ensemble – Nimbus Records 1983
The Dante Troubadours: Martin Best Mediaeval Ensemble – Nimbus Records 1982
A Medieval Christmas – Innovative Music 1986
A Dance in the Garden of Mirth: Dufay Collective – Chandos 1994
Dances from Terpsichore: Michael Praetorius – London: L'Oiseau Lyre 1986
Spem in alium, Sacred Choral Works: Thomas Tallis – Chandos 1990
1588 Music from the Time of the Armada: York Waits – Wotton-under-Edge 1988
Let's Make Tudor Music: Lucie and Roddy Skeaping – Stainer and Bell 1996

Baroque (seventeenth and eighteenth centuries)
The Four Seasons: Antonio Vivaldi – RCA 1987
Water Music and Royal Fireworks Music: George Frederik Handel – Benelux: Disk 1991
Baroque Masterpieces and Essential Classics – Sony 2002, includes:
    Trumpet Voluntary: Jeremiah Clark
    Arrival of the Queen of Sheba: Handel, George Frederick
    Jesu Joy of Man's Desiring: Johann Sebastian Bach
    Adagio: Thomaso Albinoni
    Canon: Johann Pachelbel

Classical (late eighteenth century)
Flute and Harp Concerto: Wolfgang Amadeus Mozart – Colchester: Chandos 1992
Horn Concerto no.3: Wolfgang Amadeus Mozart – Deutsche Grammophon 1990
Baroque Masterpieces and Essential Classics
    Dance of the Blessed Spirits: Christoph Willibald Gluck

Romantic (nineteenth century)
Pictures at an Exhibition: Modest Mussorgsky – RCA Victor 1992
The Victorian Music Hall – Hampton Wick 1995
Hebrides Overture: Felix Mendelssohn – Hamburg: DGG 1971
The Sorcerer's Apprentice: Dukas, Paul – Denon 1993

Modern (early twentieth century)
The Rite of Spring: Igor Stravinsky – Colchester 1995
Thus Spake Zarathustra: Richard Strauss – Sony 1963
Rhapsody in Blue: George Gershwin – Colchester: Chandos 1992
Lieutenant Kije, March and The Love of Three Oranges: Serge Prokofiev – Naxos 1995
Appalachian Spring; Variations on a Shaker Hymn: Aaron Copeland – Sony
Sea Interludes from Peter Grimes: Benjamin Britten – Nimbus Records 1994

Post-modern (late twentieth and twenty first centuries)
The Chairman Dances: John Adams – Nonesuch 1987
Fearful Symmetries: John Adams – Nonesuch 1987
Different Trains: Steve Reich, Kronos Quartet – Nonesuch Records 2005

General
Guild of Ancient Fifes and Drums: By Beat of Drum – London: Bandlea 1987
Classic FM Hall of Fame 2000 – Classic FM Records 2000
Children's Classics – Karussell 1993
Preludes, Airs and Yodels: Penguin Café EG Records 1981
Walking in the Air in *The Snowman*: Howard Blake – CBS Records
Drumming Catalyst: Evelyn Glennie (performer) – BMG Music 1996
Halleluia: Shrek the movie – 2001

Nursery rhymes

Nursery Rhymes sung by Debi Gliori – Red House Books DGR2

Music with strong character

Excitement
Carmina Burana: Carl Orff – EMI Classics 2001

Fanfare
Sinfonietta: Leos Janácek – EMI Classics 1994

Dance
Les Sylphides: Frederik Chopin – Philips
The Nutcracker: Tchaikovsky P. I. 19 cent. – Austria: Sony 1993

Space
Space Themes – UK: Tring International 1990
Star Wars, Saga: John Williams: Phillips 1999

Offbeat jazz
Take Five: Dave Brubeck 1954/1966 – Columbia 1993

Atmospheric
Kundon (from the film): Philip Glass – Nonesuch Records 1997
Adiemus: Karl Jenkins – Virgin Records 1995
The Mission: Ennio Morricone: Virgin Records 1992

Appendix 6
Referencing to the Professional Standards for QTS

1. Professional attributes	1	Have high expectations of children and young people including a commitment to ensuring that they can achieve their full educational potential and to establishing fair, respectful, trusting, supportive and constructive relationships with them.	Use music activity to develop effective relationships between children. Music ensemble work requires taking turns and being sensitive to others.
	2	Demonstrate the positive values, attitudes and behaviour they expect from children and young people.	Model a positive attitude to music making.
	3	(a) Be aware of the professional duties of teachers and the statutory framework within which they work.	
		(b) Be aware of the policies and practices of the workplace and share in collective responsibility for their implementation.	Joining in the school musical activities where possible. Implement the music policy where appropriate.
	4	Communicate effectively with children, young people, colleagues, parents and carers.	Give clear instructions. Lead music in an enthusiastic and encouraging manner.
	5	Recognise and respect the contribution that colleagues, parents and carers can make to the development and well-being of children and young people and to raising their levels of attainment.	
	6	Have a commitment to collaboration and co-operative working.	Work with other staff on co-operative music events.
	7	(a) Reflect on and improve their practice, and take responsibility for identifying and meeting their developing professional needs.	As in all subjects, evaluate and improve music teaching through reflection and identifying needs.
		(b) Identify priorities for their early professional development in the context of induction.	
	8	Have a creative and constructively critical approach towards innovation, being prepared to adapt their practice where benefits and improvements are identified.	Knowledge of the music curriculum. Being responsive to information and guidance from the music curriculum leader.
	9	Act upon advice and feedback and be open to coaching and mentoring.	Respond to written and verbal feedback on music lessons.

2. Professional knowledge and understanding	10	Have a knowledge and understanding of teaching, learning and behaviour management strategies ...	Listening to music as a management strategy. All such strategies help to make the classroom a safe and well ordered environment.
	11	(b) Be informed of a range of approaches to assessment, including the importance of formative assessment.	Appraising: the role of children's self and peer evaluation in music.
	12	Have a secure knowledge and understanding of their subjects/curriculum areas to enable them to teach effectively across the age and ability range for which they are trained to teach.	Knowledge of music genres in broad terms. Knowledge of a range of teaching and learning strategies to encourage attentive and thoughtful listening.
	13	Know and understand the relevant and non-statutory curricula...and other relevant initiatives across the age and ability range for which they are trained to teach.	Check how the knowledge and understanding in this section relates to the National Curriculum.
	14	Have a secure knowledge and understanding of their subjects/curriculum areas and related pedagogy to enable them to teach effectively across the age and ability range for which they are trained.	Have good knowledge of the music curriculum and some strategies to implement it with the classes being taught in placements.
	15	Know and understand the relevant statutory and non-statutory curricula, frameworks, including those provided through the National Strategies, for their subjects/curriculum areas, and other relevant initiatives applicable to the age and ability range for which they are trained.	
	16	Have passed the professional skills tests in numeracy, literacy and information and communication technology (ICT).	
	17	Know how to use skills in literacy, numeracy and ICT to support their teaching and wider professional activities.	
	18	Understand how children and young people develop and that the progress and well-being of learners are affected by a range of developmental, social, religious, ethnic, cultural and linguistic influences.	Know something of how children develop musically and have informed expectations of them. Be aware of different cultural attitudes to music and how to accommodate these.
	19	Know how to make effective personalised provision for those they teach, including those for whom English is an additional language or who have special educational needs or disabilities, and how to take practical account of diversity and promote equality and inclusion in their teaching.	Consider the contribution music can make to a fully inclusive classroom.

	20	Know and understand the roles of colleagues with specific responsibilities, including those with responsibility for learners with special educational needs and disabilities and other individual learning needs.	
	21	Make effective use of a range of assessment, monitoring and recording strategies.	Appraising: the role of children's self and peer evaluation in music. Teacher's appraisal.
3. Professional skills	22	Provide timely, accurate and constructive feedback on learners' attainment, progress and areas for development.	Appraising: the role of children's self and peer evaluation in music. Teacher's appraisal.
	23	Design opportunities for learners to develop their literacy, numeracy and ICT skills.	Include keyboards and/or computer software when appropriate.
	24	Plan homework or other out-of-class work to sustain learners' progress and to extend and consolidate their learning.	Incorporate skills acquired in extra-curricular music-making in class music where possible.
	25	Teach lessons and sequences of lessons across the age and ability range for which they are trained in which they:	Plan coherent and progressive units of work.
		(a) use a range of teaching strategies and resources, including e-learning, taking practical account of diversity and promoting equality and inclusion;	Make use of instrumental resources when appropriate.
		(b) build on prior knowledge, develop concepts and processes, enable learners to apply new knowledge, understanding and skills and meet learning objectives;	Make planning in music progressive especially in the development of skills.
		(c) adapt their language to suit the learners they teach, introducing new ideas and concepts clearly, and using explanations, questions, discussions and plenaries effectively;	Make sure children understand the basic music terminology and can use this to appraise their work.
		(d) manage the learning of individuals, groups and whole classes, modifying their teaching to suit the stage of the lesson.	Consider where different kinds of grouping will be effective especially for composing work.
	26	(a) Make effective use of a range of assessment, monitoring and recording strategies.	Monitor while teaching. Use children's own assessments through self appraisal.
		(b) Assess the learning needs of those they teach in order to set challenging learning objectives.	
	27	Provide timely, accurate and constructive feedback on learners' attainment, progress and areas for development.	Use positive feedback to maintain children's confidence but use directed praise to support objectives.

	28	Support and guide learners to reflect on their learning, identify the progress they have made and identify their emerging learning needs.	Use children's own appraisal in plenaries.
	29	Evaluate the impact of their teaching on the progress of all learners, and modify their planning and classroom practice where necessary.	Reflect on lessons taught and modify appropriately.
	30	Establish a purposeful and safe learning environment conducive to learning and identify opportunities for learners to learn in out of school contexts.	Music requires careful organisation: <ul><li>distribution of instruments;</li><li>organisation of group work and particularly activities involving noise and movement.</li></ul>
	31	Establish a clear framework for classroom discipline to manage learners' behaviour constructively and promote their self-control and independence.	
	32	Work as a team member and identify opportunities for working with colleagues, sharing the development of effective practice with them.	
	33	Ensure that colleagues working with them are appropriately involved in supporting learning and understand the roles they are expected to fulfil.	Plan for the use of assistants to support music lessons.

Appendix 7
Referencing to Every Child Matters

Being healthy	Emotional and physical well-being	Responses to music are emotional and through appraisal increase emotional awareness or intelligence. Class performance and particularly singing help to maintain a sense of well-being in the class and in children's lives in general.
Staying safe	Protection from harm and neglect	Listening to music as a management strategy. All such strategies help to make the classroom a safe and well-ordered environment. Children learn self discipline through the disciplines of musical performance.
Enjoying and achieving	Education, training and recreation	All musical activities in school, both those with an educational emphasis and social aspects of performance.
Making a contribution	The contribution made by them to society	Performing in school. Performing to others outside school.
Economic well-being	Social and economic well-being	Music as a socially satisfying activity especially for those who lack social confidence. Awareness that music can offer a career option.

Index

Added to the page reference, 'f' denotes a figure and 'g' denotes the glossary.